Continuum Studies
Research in Education

MAY 2023

Series editor: Richard Andrews

Teaching and Learning
Design and Technology

Related titles:

Richard Andrews: *Teaching and Learning English*
Bill Gillham: *The Research Interveiw*
Bill Gillham: *Developing a Questionnaire*
Bill Gillham: *Case Study Research Methods*
Richard Hickman: *Art Education 11–18*
Helen Nicholson: *Teaching Drama 11–18*
Marilyn Nickson: *Teaching and Learning Mathematics*
Adrian Oldknow and Ron Taylor: *Teaching Mathematics with ICT*
Richard Pring: *Philosophy of Educational Research*

Teaching and Learning Design and Technology

A guide to recent research and its applications

Edited by John Eggleston

CONTINUUM
London and New York

Continuum

The Tower Building   370 Lexington Avenue
11 York Road   New York
London SE1 7NX   NY 10017-6503

First published 2000

British Library Cataloguing-in-Publication Data

A catalogue record for this book is available from the British Library.

ISBN   0-8264-4753-8

Designed and typeset by Ben Cracknell Studios
Printed and bound in Great Britain by Biddles Ltd, Guildford and King's Lynn

Contents

Contributors

David Barlex directs the Nuffield Design and Technology Project. He taught science and design and technology in comprehensive schools for 14 years. He lectured in education at Goldsmiths College, University of London, for five years. He has written widely for both science and design and technology education. He is currently a senior lecturer at the Faculty of Education, Brunel University. His special interests are curriculum development and the professional development of teachers.

Clare Benson has worked in primary schools both in this country and overseas and in the advisory services of a local education authority, prior to her appointment at the University of Central England where she is Director of the School of Mathematics, Science and Technology and of the Centre for Research in Primary Technology (CRIPT). She has spoken at national and international conferences, and written numerous papers, articles and books relating to design and technology.

John Cave is Professor of Technology Education at Middlesex University and contributes there to 'mainstream' teacher education as well as externally funded projects – notably Gatsby's Technology Enhancement Programme. He has been extensively involved in INSET over a number of years and has written or edited over 40 books for peer review and student use. His principal interest is in the development of teaching resources, materials and equipment for the technology curriculum and he was a founder member of the Technology Education Centre at

Middlesex University. He has served in an advisory capacity for the DfEE, QCA, NCVQ, examination boards and many other organizations.

John Eggleston is Visiting Professor of Education at Middlesex University. He has played a leading role in research and development in design and technology education as leader of the Keele Project from 1967–73 and a wide spectrum of subsequent projects. He is author of a range of books on design and technology and founded and edited *Design and Technology Teaching*. Currently he is Vice Chair and Treasurer of the Design and Technology Association and Chair of the Judges of the Young Electronic Designer Awards.

Ian Holdsworth is a senior lecturer at Middlesex University where he leads the PGCE course in design and technology education. Previous to this he worked in a range of manufacturing industries before teaching in secondary schools. He is an experienced crafts person, teacher and author with a variety of subject interests including the history of plastics.

Rob Johnsey lectures in primary school design and technology and science in the Institute of Education, Warwick University. He has taught in secondary and primary schools both in this country and abroad and has led a wide range of teacher in-service courses in science and design and technology. He first began publishing books for teachers while he was a middle school teacher in the mid-1980s, writing about ideas he had developed alongside teachers in his own school. He is a member of the Association for Science Education and an active member of the Primary Advisory Group for the Design and Technology Association.

Richard Kimbell is Professor of Technology Education at Goldsmiths College, University of London. He has taught design and technology in schools and been course director for undergraduate and postgraduate courses of teacher education. He founded the Technology Education Research Unit (TERU) in 1990 and is resonsible for research projects and research students in the design department.

Soo Miller taught science – and was a headmistress – in London schools before moving to Goldsmiths College to join the TERU research team. She is responsible for administering all research projects and was the principal research officer on the Design Council project on which her contribution to Chapter 9 is based.

John Saxton taught design and technology in Cambridgeshire before moving to Goldsmiths College, University of London to join the APU research team. He now heads the design and technology PGCE course and is a key member of TERU, supporting research projects including the Design Council project on which Chapter 9 is based.

George Shield is Director of the School of Education at Sunderland University. After leaving Loughborough College he taught design and technology for over twenty years in a number of secondary schools before entering teacher education in 1984. His research interests focus upon the school curriculum and the teaching of technology. He has published widely on these topics and been invited to speak at a number of international meetings, most recently in Taiwan and Washington, USA.

Peter Taylor taught design and technology in a range of inner London schools. Since joining Middlesex University in 1986 he has been involved in a broad range of aspects of initial teacher education as well as design and technology in education. He has research interests in pedagogical issues within design and technology.

Richard Tufnell is currently Dean of the School of Lifelong Learning and Education and Professor of Design and Technology at Middlesex University. After a teaching career in London and Europe he became Secondary Education Officer at the Design Council before joining the then Middlesex Polytechnic in the 1980s. He has directed a number of research projects, written extensively on design and technology, led a number of curriculum initiatives both in the higher and secondary sectors of education, and developed a variety of teaching resources ranging from textbooks to CD-ROMs and teaching kits. His research interests include the assessment of design and technology, issues relating to communication skills and techniques and education in the workplace.

Series editor's introduction

The function and role of the series

The need for the series

Internationally, the gap between research, policy and practice in public life has become a matter of concern. When professional practice – in nursing, education, local governance and other fields – is uninformed by research, it tends to reinvent itself in the light of a range of (often conflicting) principles. Research uninformed by practical considerations tends to be ignored by practitioners, however good it is academically. Similarly, the axis between policy and research needs to be a working one if each is to inform the other. Research is important to the professions, just as it is in industry and the economy: we have seen in the last fifteen years especially that companies which do not invest in research tend to become service agents for those companies that are at the cutting edge of practice. The new work order (see Gee *et al.*, 1996) makes research a necessity.

There is increasing interest in teaching as an evidence-based profession, though it is not always clear what an 'evidence-based profession' is. In the mid-1990s, in England, the Teacher Training Agency (TTA) was promoting a close link between research and the application of research in practice – for example, in the classroom. It also laid particular emphasis on teachers as researchers, seeming at the time to exclude university-based researchers from the picture. It quickly became evident, however, that research-based teaching was generally impracticable and often a diversion from the core business of teaching and learning. Furthermore, there was policy confusion as to whether the main thrust of the initiative was to encourage teachers to be researchers, or to encourage teachers to use research to improve their performance in the classroom. It is the second of these aims that gained in momentum during the late 1990s and the first part of the present century.

Teachers as users of research brought about a subtly different term: 'evidence-based practice' in an evidence-based profession. The analogy with developments in nursing education and practice were clear. David Hargreaves made the analogy in a keynote TTA lecture, speculating as to why the teaching profession was not more like the nursing and medical professions in its use of research. The analogy was inexact, but the message was clear enough: let researchers undertake education research, and let teachers apply it. With scarce resources and an increasing influence from the Department for Education and Employment (DfEE) in the formation and implementation of teachers' professional development following the 1988 paper *Teachers: Meeting the Challenge of Change,* TTA's own position on evidence-based practice was limited and more focused. In 1999–2000 the Agency initiated a series of conferences entitled 'Challenging teachers' thinking about research and evidence-based practice'. The DfEE's own paper *Professional Development* (2000) sets out for discussion the place of research within teachers' professional development, including the announcement of best practice research scholarships for serving teachers:

> We are keen to support teachers using and carrying out research, which is a valuable way to build knowledge and understanding about raising standards of teaching and learning. Research can have advantages for the individual teacher; for their school; and for other schools in sharing lessons learned. We believe that research can be a particularly valuable activity for experienced teachers. (p. 25)

Part of the function of the present series is to provide ready access to the evidence base for busy teachers, teacher-researchers, parents and governors in order to help them improve teaching which, in turn, will improve learning and raise standards. But it is worth discussing here what the evidence base is for teaching a school subject, and how it might be applied to the acts of teaching and learning.

Evidence is inert. It needs not so much application as *transformation* in order to make learning happen in the classroom. That transformation requires the teacher to weigh up the available evidence, devise pedagogical approaches to be included in an overall teaching programme for a year, term, week or unit of work and then to put those approaches into action. Evidence can inform both the planning and the actual delivery. Imagine yourself in the middle of teaching a class about differences between spoken standard English and a number of dialects. You can draw on the evidence to help you plan and teach the lesson, but you will also need to depend on the evidence in order to improvise, adapt and meet particular learning needs *during* the course of the lesson.

The gaps between policy, research and practice

In February 2000, in a possibly unprecedented gesture, the British Secretary of State for Education addressed a community of education researchers about the importance of its research for the development of government policy (DfEE, 2000). The basic message was that research, policy and practice needed to be in closer relation to each other in order to maximize the benefits of each. During the 1980s and 1990s, the gap between research and policy was chasm-like. Politicians and other policy-makers tended to choose research evidence to support their own prejudices about education policy. A clear case was the affirmation of the value of homework by successive governments in the face of research which suggested homework had little or no effect on the performance of pupils. Similarly, the gap between research and practice was often unbridged. One problem facing the education sector as a whole is that research moves to a different rhythm than policy or practice. Longitudinal research may take ten or fifteen years to gestate; policy moves in four-year cycles, according to governments and elections; practice is often interested in a short-term fix.

The creation of a National Education Research Forum in late 1999 goes some way to informing policy with research. Its function is very much to inform policy rather than to inform practice, and its remit is much larger than a focus on schooling. But its creation, along with the emergence of series such as the present one and websites which aim to mediate between research and practice can only improve the relationship between research, policy and practice. A virtuous triangle is slowly taking shape.

The focus on subjects at early years, primary/elementary and secondary/high school levels

The series is built around subjects. At the time of going to press, there are titles on English, mathematics, science, design and technology, modern foreign languages and economics and business studies either published or in the pipeline. Further titles will be added in due course. All but one of these subjects applies to primary/elementary and secondary/high school levels; one of the aims of the series is to ensure that research in the teaching and learning of school subjects is not confined by phase, but is applicable from the early years through to the end of compulsory education.

The focus on subjects is a pragmatic one. Although there is considerable pressure to move away from an essentially nineteenth-century conception of the curriculum as divided into disciplines and subjects, the current National Curriculum in England and Wales, and curricula elsewhere in the world, are still largely designed on the basis of subjects. The research we have drawn on in the making of the present series therefore derives from the core discipline, the school subject and the teaching of the school subject in each case. Where other research is contributory to practice, we have not stopped at including it (for example the work of the social psychologist Vygotsky in relation to the teaching of English) so that each book is an interpretation by the author(s) of the significance of research to teaching and learning within the subject. With some subjects, the research literature is vast and the authors have made what they take to be appropriate selections for the busy teacher or parent; with other subjects, there is less material to draw on and the tendency has been to use what research there is, often carried out by the author or authors themselves.

We take it that research into the development of learning in a subject at primary school level will be of interest to secondary school teachers, and vice versa. The books will also provide a bridge between phases of education, seeing the development of learning as a continuous activity.

The international range

The series is international in scope. It aims not only to draw on research undertaken in a range of countries across the world in order to get at the best evidence possible; it will also apply to different systems across the world because of its attempt to get at the bedrock of good teaching and learning. References to particular education systems are kept to a minimum, and are only used when it is necessary to illuminate the context of the research. Where possible, comparative research is referred to.

Such an international perspective is important for a number of reasons: first, because research is sometimes carried out internationally; second, because globalization in learning is raising questions about the basis of new approaches to learning; third, because different perspectives can enhance the overall sense of what works best in different contexts. The series is committed to such diversity, both in drawing on research across the world and in serving the needs of learners and teachers across the world.

The time frame for the research

In general, the series looks at research from the 1960s to the present. Some of the most significant research in some subjects was undertaken in the 60s. In the 1990s, the advent of the Internet and the World Wide Web has meant that the research toolkit has been increased. It is now possible to undertake literature reviews online and via resources in formats such as CD-ROM, as well as via the conventional print formats of journals and books. The books cannot claim to be comprehensive; at the same time each is an attempt to represent the best of research in particular fields for the illumination of teaching and learning.

The nature of applied research in education

Applied research, as a term, needs some explication. It can mean both research into the application of 'blue-skies' research, theory or ideas in the real-world contexts of the classroom or other site of education and learning; and it can also mean research that arises from such contexts. It sometimes includes action research because of the close connection to real-world contexts. It is distinctly different from desk-based research, 'blue-skies' research or research into the history, policy or socio-economics of education as a discipline. There is further exploration of different kinds of research in the next section. Here I want to set out why applied research cannot be fully disconnected from other kinds of research, and to demonstrate the unity and inter-connectedness of research approaches in education.

Research has to be 'academic' in the sense of the *disinterested* pursuit of truth (to the extent that truth is an absolute). If the research does not attempt to be as objective as it can be (within the paradigm which it adopts – which may be a subjective one), it cannot be taken seriously.

Second, research – like practice – has to be informed by theory. There is little point in undertaking action research or empirical research without a clear sense of its underlying assumptions and ideologies. Theory, too, needs to be examined to ensure that it supports or challenges practice and convention. A research cycle may require full treatment of each of the following phases of research:

- definition of the problem or research question; or positing of a hypothesis;
- review of the theory underpinning the field or fields in which the empirical research is to be undertaken;
- devising of an apppropriate methodology to solve the problem, answer the research question or test the hypothesis;
- empirical work with qualitative and/or quantitative outcomes;
- analysis and discussion of results;
- conclusion and implications for practice and further research.

The stages of conventional research, outlined above, might be undertaken as part of a three-year full-time or five- to six-year part-time research degree; or they might form the basis of an action research cycle (at its simplest, 'plan-do-review'). Although the cycle as a whole is important, research is not invalidated if it undertakes one or more stages or elements of the cycle. For example, research which undertook to cover the first two stages in a thorough examination of the literature on a particular topic could be very useful research; similarly, research which aimed to test an existing theory (or even replicate an earlier study in a new context) – the fourth, fifth and sixth stages as outlined above – might also be very useful research.

It is a mistake to think that research must be immediately applicable. If we think of one of the most influential research projects of the last 30 years – Barnes *et al.*'s work on talk in classrooms in the late 1960s for example – we would note in this case that its impact might not be felt fully until fifteen years later (in the introduction of compulsory testing of oral competence in English (in England and Wales) in 1986).

In short, a large cycle over a number of years can be as important (it is often more so) than a short action research cycle over a year or two. We do need further research into how teachers actually change and improve their practice before we can make too many assumptions about the practical value of research.

Different kinds of research

Different kinds of research can be identified. They are:

1. theoretical, historical and strategic research;
2. applied research (including evaluation, consultancy);
3. research for and about learning and teaching;
4. scholarship.

These categories are not perfect; categories rarely are. Nor are they exclusive.

Theoretical and historical research

These kinds of research, along with strategic research, do not have immediate practical application. Their importance is undiminished in the light of a gradual shift towards the impact of research and the presence of 'users' on Research Assessment Exercise panels.[1] In the 1990s, there was a gradual widening of the definition of research to include artefacts and other patentable inventions.

The following definition of research is both catholic and precise:

'Research' for the purpose of the research assessment exercise is to be understood as original investigation undertaken in order to gain knowledge and understanding. It includes work of direct relevance to the needs of commerce and industry, as well as to the public and voluntary sectors; scholarship; the invention and generation of ideas, images, performances and artefacts including design, where these lead to new or substantially improved insights; and the use of existing knowledge in experimental development to produce new or substantially improved materials, devices, products and processes, including design and construction. It excludes routine testing and analysis of materials, components and processes, e.g. for the maintenance of national standards, as distinct from the development of new analytical techniques. It also excludes the development of teaching materials that do not embody original research.

(HEFCE, 1998)

Applied research, including evaluation and consultancy

Much research may be of an applied kind. That is to say, it might include:

- research arising from classroom and school needs;
- research undertaken in schools, universities and other workplaces;
- research which takes existing knowledge and applies or tests it in different contexts;
- research through knowledge and technology transfer;
- collaborations with industry, other services (e.g. health), arts organizations and other bodies concerned with improving learning and the economy in the region and beyond;
- evaluation;
- consultancies that include a research dimension; and
- the writing of textbooks and other works designed to improve learning, as long as these textbooks are underpinned by research and there is evidence of such research.

The common factor in these approaches is that they are all designed to improve learning in the different fields in which they operate, and thus to inform teaching, training and other forms of education.

Research for and about learning and teaching

Research into the processes of learning is often interdisciplinary. It might include:

- fundamental enquiry into learning processes;
- research into a region's educational needs;
- the creation of a base of applied research to underpin professional practice;

- the establishment of evidence for the provision of specific pedagogic materials;
- the development of distance-learning techniques, materials and modes of delivery; and
- examination of cases of cutting-edge learning.

Research *for* learning means research designed to improve the quality of learning; in some quarters, it is referred to as 'research and development'. It is a well-known and well-used approach in the making of new products. The writing of school textbooks and other forms of publication for the learning market, whether in print or electronic form, qualifies as research for learning if there is evidence of research underpinning it. Such research is valuable in that it works toward the creation of a new product or teaching programme.

Research *about* learning is more conventional within academic research cultures. It is represented in a long-standing tradition with the cognitive sciences, education, sociology and other disciplines. Such research does and should cover learning in informal and formal settings. Research for learning should be grounded in research about learning.

Scholarship

Scholarship can be defined as follows: 'scholarship [is] defined as the creation, development and maintenance of the intellectual infrastructure of subjects and disciplines, in forms such as dictionaries, scholarly editions, catalogues and contributions to major research databases' (HEFCE RAE paper 1/98, p. 40). But there is more to scholarship than this. As well as supporting and maintaining the intellectual infrastructure of subjects and disciplines, scholarship is a practice and an attitude of mind. It concerns the desire for quality, accuracy and clarity in all aspects of learning; the testing of hunches and hypotheses against rigorous evidence; the identification of different kinds of evidence for different purposes (e.g. for the justification of the arts in the curriculum). It also reflects a quest for excellence in design of the written word and other forms of communication in the presentation of knowledge.

Teacher research

One aspect of the move to put research into the hands of its subjects or respondents has been the rise of practitioner research. Much of the inspiration for this kind of research has come from the work of Donald Schön on the reflective practitioner (e.g. Schön, 1987) in the 1980s. Practitioner research puts the practitioner centre stage and in its purest form the research is directed, undertaken and evaluated by the practitioners themselves. In less pure forms it is facilitated by outside researchers who nevertheless make sure that the needs and ideas of the practitioners are central to the progress of the research. Teacher research or 'teachers as researchers' is one particular manifestation of this movement. Key books are those by Webb (1990) and Webb and Vulliamy (1992).

The advantages of teacher research are that it is usually close to the concerns of the classroom, its empirical work is carried out in the classroom and the benefits of the research can be seen most immediately in the classroom. Most often it takes the form of action research with the aim of improving practice. When the research is of a rigorous nature, it includes devices such as a pre-test (a gauging of the state of play before an experiment is undertaken), the experimental period (in which, for example, a new method of teaching a particular aspect of a subject is tried) and post-test (a gauging of the state of play at the end of the experimental period). Sometimes more scientifically based approaches, like the use of a control group to compare the effects on an experimental group, are used. Disadvantages include the fact that unless such checks and balances are observed, the experiments are likely to become curriculum development rather than research, with no clear means of evaluating their worth or impact. Furthermore, changes can take place without a sense of what the state of play was beforehand, or how far the changes have had an effect.

In the second half of the 1990s, the TTA in England and Wales initiated two programmes that gave more scope for teachers to undertake research themselves rather than be the users or subjects of it. The Teacher Research Grant Scheme and the School-Based Research Consortia enabled a large number of teachers and four consortia to undertake research. Much of it is cited in this series, and all of it has been consulted. Not all this kind of research has led to masters' or doctoral work in universities, but a large number of teachers have undertaken dissertations and theses across the world to answer research questions and test hypotheses about aspects of education. Again, we have made every effort to track down and represent research of this kind. One of the criticisms made by the TTA in the late 1990s was that much of this latter academic research was neither applicable nor was applied to the classroom. This criticism may have arisen from a misunderstanding about the scope, variety and nature of education research, discussed in the section on the nature of applied research above.

The applicability of academic research work to teaching

This section deals with the link between masters' and doctoral research, as conducted by students in universities, and its applicability to teaching. The section takes a question-and-answer format[2]. The first point to make is about the nature of dissemination. Dissemination does not only take place at the end of a project. In many projects (action research, research and development) dissemination takes place along the way, e.g. in networks that are set up, databases of contacts, seminars, conferences, in-service education, etc. Many of these seminars and conferences include teachers (e.g. subject professional conferences).

What arrangements would encourage busy education departments, teachers, researchers and their colleagues to collaborate in the dissemination of good quality projects likely to be of interest and use to classroom teachers? What would make teachers enthusiastic about drawing their work to the attention of colleagues?

Good dissemination is partly a result of the way a research project is set up. Two examples will prove the point: one from The University of Hull and one from Middlesex University.

Between 1991 and 1993 an action research project was undertaken by The University of Hull's (then) School of Education to improve the quality of argument in ten primary and ten secondary schools in the region. Teachers collaborated with university lecturers to set up mini-projects in each of the schools. These not only galvanized interest among other teachers in each of the schools, but made for considerable exchange between the participating schools. Much dissemination (probably reaching at least 200 teachers in the region) took place *during* the project. Conventional *post hoc* dissemination in the form of articles and presentations by teachers took place after the project.

In early 1998, Middlesex University, through the TTA's in-service education and training (INSET) competition, won funding in collaboration with the London Boroughs of Enfield and Barnet to run INSET courses from September 1998. Alongside the INSET courses themselves, four MPhil/PhD studentships were awarded for teachers to undertake longer-term evaluations of in-service curricular development. At the time (September 1998) several applicants wished to focus their research on the literacy hour. This research informed INSET activity and was of interest to teachers in the region, as well as providing summative evidence for a wider community.

In conclusion, the research projects of relevance to teachers must (a) be engaging, (b) be disseminated during the course of the research as well as after it, (c) be seen to benefit schools during the research as well as after it, and (d) involve as large a number of teachers in the activity of the project as possible. Diffidence about research is seldom felt if there is involvement in it.

How can we encourage more pedagogic research with a focus on both teaching and learning?

Research into learning often has implications for teaching; and it is difficult in disciplined research to have two foci. Indeed such bifocal research may not be able to sustain its quality. Inevitably, any research into teaching must take into account the quality and amount of learning that takes place as a result of the teaching. Research into *learning* is again a pressing need. Having said that, research with a focus on *teaching* needs to be encouraged.

Would it be beneficial to build a requirement for accessible summaries into teacher research programmes? Given the difficulties involved in this process, what training or support would be needed by education researchers?

The ability to summarize is an important skill; so is the ability to write accessibly. Not all teachers or teacher researchers (or academics for that matter) have such abilities. Such requirements need not be problematical, however, nor need much attention. Teacher researchers must simply be required to provide accessible summaries of their work, whether these are conventional abstracts (often no longer than 300 words) or longer summaries of their research. Their supervisors and the funding agency must ensure that such summaries are forthcoming and are well written.

Where higher degree study by teachers is publicly funded, should teachers be required to consider from the start how their work might involve colleagues and be made accessible to other teachers?

Making a researcher consider from the start how their work might involve colleagues and be made accessible to other teachers is undesirable for a number of reasons. First, it might skew the research; second, it will put the emphasis on dissemination and audience rather than on the research itself. Part of the nature of research is that the writer must have his or her focus on the material gathered or the question examined, not on what he or she might say. This is why writing up research is not necessarily like writing a book; a thesis must be true to its material, whereas a book must speak to its audience. There is a significant difference in the two genres, which is why the translation of thesis into book is not always as easy as it might seem. Third, what is important 'from the start' is the framing of a clear research question, the definition of a problem or the positing of a testable hypothesis.

In summary, as far as teacher research and the use of findings in MA and PhD work go, there are at least the following main points which need to be addressed:

- further research on how teachers develop and improve their practice;
- exploration and exposition of the links between theory and practice;
- an understanding that dissemination is not always most effective 'after the event';
- an appreciation of the stages of a research project, and of the value of work that is not immediately convertible into practice;
- further exploration of the links between teaching and learning.

Research is not the same as evaluation

It is helpful to distinguish between research and evaluation for the purposes of the present series. Research is the critical pursuit of truth or new knowledge through enquiry; or, to use a now obsolete but nevertheless telling definition from the eighteenth century, research in music is the seeking out of patterns of harmony which, once discovered, can be applied in the piece to be played afterwards. In other words, research is about discovery of new patterns, new explanations for data – or the testing of existing theories against new data – which can inform practice.

Evaluation is different. One can evaluate something without researching it or using research techniques. But formal evaluation of education initiatives often requires the use of research approaches to determine the exact nature of the developments that have taken place or the value and worth of those developments. Evaluation almost always assumes critical detachment and the disinterested weighing up of strengths and weaknesses. It should always be sensitive to the particular aims of a project and should try to weigh the aims against the methods and results, judging the appropriateness of the methods and the validity and effect (or likely effect) of the results. It can be formative or summative: formative when it works alongside the project it is evaluating, contributing to its development in a critical, dispassionate way; and summative when it is asked to identify at the end of a project the particular strengths and weaknesses of the approach.

Evaluation can use any of the techniques and methods that research uses in order to gather and analyse data. For example, an evaluation of the strengths and weaknesses of the Teacher Training Agency's School-Based Research Consortia could use formal questionnaires, semi-structured interviews and case studies of individual teacher's development to assess the impact of the consortia. Research methods that provide quantitative data (largely numerical) or qualitative data (largely verbal) could be used.

Essentially, the difference between research and evaluation comes down to a difference in function: the function of research is to discover new knowledge via a testing of hypothesis, the answering of a research question or the solving of a problem – or indeed the creation of a hypothesis, the asking of a question or the formulating or exploring of a problem. The function of evaluation is simply to evaluate an existing phenomenon.

How to access, read and interpret research

The series provides a digest of the best and most relevant research in the teaching and learning of school subjects. Each of the authors aims to mediate between the plethora of research in the field and the needs of the busy teacher, headteacher, adviser, parent or governor who wants to know how best to improve practice in teaching in order to improve standards in learning. In other words, much of the work of seeking out research and interpreting it is done for you by the authors of the individual books in the series.

At the same time, the series is intended to help you to access and interpret research more generally. Research is continuing all the time; it is impossible for a book series, however comprehensive, to cover all research or to present the very latest research in a particular field.

In order to help you access, read and interpret research the following guidelines might help:

- How clear is the research question or problem or hypothesis?
- If there is more than one question or problem, can you identify a main question or problem as opposed to subsidiary ones? Does the researcher make the distinction clear?
- Is any review of the literature included? How comprehensive is it? How critical is it of past research? Does it, for instance, merely cite previous literature to make a new space for itself? Or does it build on existing research?
- Determine the size of the sample used in the research. Is this a case study of a particular child or a series of interviews with, say, ten pupils, or a survey of tens or hundreds of pupils? The generalizability of the research will depend on its scale and range.
- Is the sample a fair reflection of the population that is being researched? For example, if all the 12- to 13-year-old pupils in a particular town are being researched (there might be 600 of them) what is the size of the sample?
- Are the methods used appropriate for the study?
- Is the data gathered appropriate for an answering of the question, testing of the hypothesis or solving of the problem?
- What conclusions, if any, are drawn? Are they reasonable?
- Is the researcher making recommendations based on sound results, or are implications for practice drawn out? Is the researcher aware of the limitations of the study?
- Is there a clear sense of what further research needs to be undertaken?

Equipped with questions like these, and guided by the authors of the books in the series, you will be better prepared to make sense of research findings and apply them to the improvement of your practice for the benefit of the students you teach. The bibliographies and references will provide you with the means of exploring the field more extensively, according to your own particular interests and needs.

Richard Andrews

References

Barnes, D., Britton, J. and Rosen, H. (1969) *Language, the Learner and the School*. Harmondsworth: Pelican.

DfEE (1998) *Teachers: Meeting the Challenge of Change*. London: HMSO.

DfEE (2000) *Professional Development*. London: Department for Education and Employment.

Gee, J. P., Hull, G. and Lankshear, C. (1996) *The New Work Order: Behind the Language of the New Capitalism*. St Leonards, NSW: Allen and Unwin.

HEFCE (1998) 'Research Assessment Exercise 2001: key decisions and issues for further consultation'. Paper to Higher Education Funding Council for England, January, 40.

Schön, D. (1987) *Educating the Reflective Practitioner*. San Francisco: Jossey-Bass.

Webb, R. (ed.) (1990) *Practitioner Research in the Primary School*. London: Falmer.

Webb, R. and Vulliamy, G. (1992) *Teacher Research and Special Educational Needs*. London: David Fulton.

Notes

1   The Research Assessment Exercise, conducted by the Higher Education Funding Council For England, was undertaken at four- or five-year intervals between 1986 and 2001 and may or may not take place in the middle of the first decade of the century. Its aim is to gauge the quality of research produced by research institutions around the UK in order to attribute funding in subsequent years. Critics of the exercise have suggested that, despite attempts to make it recognize the value of applied research and the applicability of research, its overall effect has been to force departments of education in universities to concentrate on producing high quality research rather than working at the interface of research and practice.

2   This section is based on a submission to the Teacher Training Agency in 1998.

Introduction

John Eggleston

Design and technology enters the new millennium as an established and necessary component of the school curriculum in most major countries across the world. Yet, more than almost any other subject, its roots are complex. They range from traditional craft cultures, manufacturing practices, new and old technologies and design processes and much else. Before the subject could be enshrined in legislation development work was necessary and took place in curriculum projects in many countries from the 1960s onwards.

Yet although many of the development studies took place in universities and other research establishments, relatively little research on design and technology teaching has been done until the past decade. This has meant that design and technology teachers have had to base their professional studies on research undertaken for other subjects. So they have had to build much of their teaching, guidance and management on approaches developed for other subjects and adapt them as best they can.

Fortunately the situation has changed. The overriding reason is, of course, the growing need for information on effective teaching as the subject expands in range, quality and complexity. But another, fortuitous reason is that most design and technology teacher training now takes place in universities where staff are very strongly urged to undertake and publish research. This has created an opportunity that did not exist previously.

This book has drawn together representatives of some of the most important research on design and technology of the last decade. Each chapter is written by the researchers and presents the findings directly, contexting them in the related areas of research for readers who wish to explore further.

Most importantly, each shows how the findings can influence readers' professional practice in fields ranging from primary schools through to higher and adult education.

Claire Benson reviews the introduction of design and technology into the primary school curriculum – for most teachers a new and unknown subject – and recalls the efforts to win the hearts and minds of teachers who take on the unfamiliar tasks required. She describes the research-led strategies to consolidate and achieve fuller understanding of the subject, the identification of teaching approaches, planning and evaluation, the interpretation of schemes of work and much else. She reviews and illustrates this vast research-led enterprise and points to continuing developments.

Rob Johnsey continues with research on primary design and technology. In this chapter he describes two linked research projects. The first used classroom observation to identify the skills used by primary school children as they designed and made simple products and led to valuable suggestions for improving classroom practice. It also provided the basis for exploring how other subjects such as science could be taught effectively by using design and technology as a vehicle for learning. This led to the second project in which trial materials were used in four primary schools, giving rise to important ways to develop cross-curricular links with design and technology.

Peter Taylor considers the role of problem solving in design and technology and reviews a range of research findings including his own. Problem solving is often adopted as an obvious teaching strategy yet it can often lead to incomplete, inefficient and frustrating experiences for students and teachers. He shows how to improve the prospects for success whilst recognizing the uncertainties in any open-ended approach.

George Shield, in a classic piece of classroom-based research, seeks to investigate what makes good design and technology teachers, how they carry out their task and the possible implications this may have for other practitioners. The research was based upon an assumption that curriculum models devised by 'experts' and 'educational philosophers' in isolation from the practice of technology education must be revised in the light of professional practice. He studied the work of technology teachers in eight secondary schools in the north-east of England. Like much research, the findings once delivered seem to have been predictable – almost 'common sense'. But this is a well-known characteristic of good research.

If good teaching is important, in design and technology more than in any other subject, good resourcing is almost equally so. In his chapter,

John Cave recognizes that the provision of physical resources is a key topic for research in design and technology. After raising fundamental issues, he presents a case study of modern resource development and points to some consequences of a resource-dependent subject for curriculum development and management.

An important element of resourcing is textbooks. In his chapter, **Ian Holdsworth** analyses design and technology textbooks. A number of textbooks are cited, drawn from a database of 120 such publications compiled after research at the National Archive for Art and Design Education held at Bretton Hall, and specifically from the Burleigh Collection of Design and Technology textbooks that the archive contains. The findings illuminate both the overt and the hidden messages conveyed by the texts – and the striking changes over time. In doing so they provide a new insight into the development and practices of present day design and technology.

One of the striking features of design and technology in Britain in recent years has been the number of projects such as the Nuffield Design and Technology Project, the Royal College of Art Schools Technology Project, and the Technology Enhancement Programme. All have involved substantial research elements. A representative example is the Nuffield Foundation's exploration of how to deliver the Qualifications and Curriculum Authority's requirement that 'pupils learn to become autonomous, creative problem solvers both as individuals and in working with others'. In his chapter, **David Barlex**, the director of the project, considers how departmental organization and children's learning can be focused to achieve these features. The chapter is divided into two parts. The first reports on the role of the individual teacher in providing effective teaching. The second part considers the relevant evidence for developing a team approach to teaching across a department.

Achievement has been a dominant feature of research in design and technology. The National Curriculum introduced in England and Wales in 1988 required that pupils' achievements should be measured and reported at regular intervals. The chapter by **Richard Tufnell** is drawn from research that investigated and developed statutory assessment strategies in design and technology at the end of Key Stage 3, normally after nine years of schooling. Consequently, expertise and resources needed to be focused on the development of assessment procedures, especially given that the National Curriculum is based on criterion referencing which only recognizes and records pupils' positive achievements. This research resulted in a number of innovative approaches to criterion referenced assessment. As a consequence, the repertoire of assessment in design and technology was significantly extended. The strategies reported in this chapter have been of value in the assessment of the subject not only in the context of the National Curriculum but also in vocational and occupational contexts.

Richard Kimbell's team's contribution is important in two ways. It emphasizes that design studies, like technology studies, are not confined to schools; they form a rapidly growing component of tertiary education. Their research findings, from a Design Council-funded project, draw attention to a worrying problem in this sector: the range of skills encompassed by tertiary level design studies is vast and growing – largely arising from the expanding nature of the subject – yet the evidence shows that this range is only incompletely recognized by tutors and remains implicit rather than explicit in the students' own self-images. The consequences are an inadequate recognition of design students' capabilities by employers and by the students themselves – with negative consequences for all concerned and the subject itself. This chapter will help tutors to articulate the range of skills to the advantage of students and employers. The parallel with school design and technology studies will not be missed by readers.

The final chapter brings together the consideration of design and technology in schools, tertiary education and the adult world. The research sprang from the British Crafts Council's realization that making a product, usually three-dimensional, is at the heart of design and technology: that it is the creative experience resulting in a tangible object which makes the subject different from others. For the teacher, the added dimension is the enhanced learning experience that making delivers. These features, though widely recognized by teachers in many countries, have seldom been demonstrated by research. The Council, as part of its concern with making, decided to address this elusive area and invited three major British universities to research it. This chapter reports the genesis of the project, the results of the three research teams, the overall conclusions and the ensuing recommendations for teachers, teacher trainers and the examination and curriculum bodies.

Research is an on-going process; existing findings lead to new questions and further research. All the authors are active, continuing researchers and will be ready and willing to talk with readers about research into design and technology and, hopefully, to involve readers in active participation. Good teaching and good researching go hand in hand. The consequences are beneficial to all concerned – especially the students.

Chapter 1

Ensuring Successful Curriculum Development in Primary Design and Technology

Clare Benson

A National Curriculum for Design and Technology

When the first National Curriculum for design and technology was published (DES, 1990), a majority of primary teachers felt that large parts were unintelligible, that it was not easy to access, and that there was far too much content to cover at both Key Stages. Whilst teachers had been involved in the debates prior to publication, the documentation was not widely available. Nor were there extensive consultation meetings where teachers from a variety of schools and backgrounds could discuss not only the document but also the implications of translating the National Curriculum into a school curriculum. Lessons were learnt. Whilst a variety of draft and final documents was published between 1990 and 1995, it was only later that more open consultation took place and opinions from a variety of personnel were listened to. The 1995 document, *Design and Technology in the National Curriculum* (DFE, 1995), was generally well received and was certainly clearer and more manageable. Schools were able to translate this into a curriculum that gave breadth and balance and could be delivered in a reasonable amount of time. The review of the National Curriculum in 1998, *Maintaining Breadth and Balance* (QCA, 1998a) helped maintain the status quo and schools had almost nothing to change except for the emphasis which they placed on design and technology. Schools welcomed the fact that curricular changes of content were unnecessary and that they had the final decision with regard to time allocation. During the review for the 2000 National

Curriculum, more open consultation has meant that those who have wished to be involved in developing an appropriate curriculum for the new century have been able to do so. Whilst the final decision was made by the Secretary of State, the new document builds on the successes of the last ten years and schools that have well-developed curricula did not have to change their documentation radically.

Having achieved a workable curriculum appropriate for the start of the new century, it has been possible to research a variety of factors that have enabled schools to develop their own curriculum, building on an appropriate national framework. First, teachers' perceptions of the value of design and technology are identified. Having established its worth, other elements are identified which contribute to the successful development of a design and technology curriculum.

The value of design and technology

By its continued inclusion in the curriculum, policy-makers at the Department for Education and Employment (DfEE) and in government acknowledge that it is of value. Although there was considerable pressure to reduce the curriculum content for the 2000 National Curriculum, the subject was still included. The Design and Technology Association (DATA) has always supported the inclusion of the subject and its own review of the National Curriculum (1997) highlights the contribution of the subject to citizenship, literacy, numeracy, Information Communication and Technology skills (ICT) and in helping young people respect others' cultures and beliefs. OFSTED inspectors have identified its value in generating such enthusiasm, interest and enjoyment (OFSTED, 1996). From a survey covering eight long award-bearing courses for primary design and technology at the University of Central England in Birmingham (UCE), 96 per cent of the 149 teachers from seven LEAs who have attended such courses felt that the subject had great value and wanted it left in the curriculum (Benson and Johnsey, 1998) despite the areas of concern that the teachers still had over the implementation of the subject in their schools.

There are a number of aspects which make the subject valuable for children to experience. Design and technology prepares young people for their future lives, including the world of work. It provides them with a context within which they can use their literacy, numeracy and ICT. The children have to be flexible, to work in teams and listen and value others' points of view. The multidisciplinary nature of the subject provides opportunities for children to apply knowledge and understanding gained in the areas of, for example, science, mathematics, language, art and ICT. It is then that they can demonstrate a real understanding of a concept, given appropriate support from the teacher in making the links. Activities in design and technology are not value-free, but instead present a range of contexts through which children's awareness of values issues can be developed. This links with the increasing emphasis on values education through, for example, citizenship. Design and technology offers children the opportunity to recognize that others have different values which must be considered not only when making their own products, but when other designers produce products in the world outside school.

Because the subject includes practical work, discussion and thinking, design and technology activities help to foster a variety of personal qualities; more so than other subjects in the primary curriculum. Curiosity can be stimulated and creativity and originality can be enhanced as children research products that are already on the market and begin to design their own. There are opportunities for children to think about others' needs and wants and to make their own decisions. They learn to work in teams, to share ideas, to listen to others' viewpoints and to compromise.

Whilst design and technology should be taught to all primary school children and its value can be identified, it does not follow that it will be taught well or indeed taught at all. The hearts and minds of headteachers and teachers have had to be won over for successful curriculum development to take place. Unlike literacy and numeracy, design and technology is not a priority for the government, nor has it been identified as a core subject. It is the perceived value of the subject by those who are delivering it which has played a part in the way in which it has become embedded in the curriculum. However a number of other factors need to be in place. These are discussed below.

Understanding the nature of the subject and the National Curriculum context

Whilst a small minority of schools were delivering elements of the subject before 1990, none were delivering the full content of the new curriculum. Thus it was hardly surprising that the majority of teachers had little understanding of the subject and the content which they were expected to cover. Much debate about its nature did take place but it was generally amongst those who were not classroom-based and the outcomes did not reach the majority of classroom teachers. It is perhaps this factor alone which hindered the initial progress of its development. Rudduck (1989) argues together with others such as Aoki (1984) and Fullan (1989) that to bring about successful change there needs to be a shared understanding between group members. Furthermore, Marris (1993) cites a range of programmes intended to bring about reforms in the American school system which did not realize their intended reforms since they did not draw together teachers, children and parents to achieve mutual understanding and collaboration. Therefore it is important that a whole staff including the headteacher, non-teaching assistants and governors share a similar understanding of the nature of the subject. It is evident from INSET work that schools which have this shared understanding make progress with planning and imple-mentation. The understanding can be gained in different ways. The coordinator might attend a course and then cascade understanding to the whole staff, including non-teaching assistants, at staff meetings. Discussion is an important element of this approach as staff need to clarify their ideas in order to come to a shared understanding. An outside provider may attend a staff meeting which focuses on a discussion about the nature of the subject and the National Curriculum requirements. A member of staff who has an understanding of the subject, who may be the coordinator, might lead a staff discussion and provide a short paper as a framework for the session. Further discussions with children, parents and governors are needed to try to ensure that all those involved in the children's education understand why the subject is important and what it involves. A variety of strategies have been used to achieve this. Schools have held open evenings, assemblies, activity afternoons and design and technology weeks, and have planned activities in which all parties have participated. Displays have been created and placed where all can see. Leaflets, including examples of children's work, have been produced so that there is paper evidence of achievements and additional support for practical activities. One successful project is where children and parents come together out of school to take part in activities, supported by Initial Teacher Training students (Webster, 1999). However the debate is conducted, the result needs to have the same outcome – that of a shared understanding. Over the last ten years there have been many revisions to the National Curriculum. This has led to schools having to put aside much time to investigate the changes and interpret the effects of them on their schemes of work. Whilst many schools have found this time-consuming, there were advantages associated with the revisions. They ensured that design and technology was kept in the forefront of National Curriculum development; and the constant refinements meant that the DFE (1995) document was more manageable and easier to understand, and standards have improved more rapidly since its implementation (Ive, 1997). The new National Curriculum for 2000 (DfEE, 1999) has built on this and hopefully this document will prove equally useful for schools as they plan an appropriate curriculum for their children.

A national organization

DATA has played a positive, major role in the development of the curriculum and it is, perhaps, unusual that a national organization should be so involved. However, the organization has been invited to be part of consultations at all levels and has been very influential as decisions are made. It has provided excellent materials to support the implementation of the subject in schools; indeed it has produced the widest range of publications available at the present time. It has been involved in producing *A Scheme of Work for Key Stages 1 and 2: Design and Technology* (QCA, 1998b), the first national exemplar scheme which was based on DATA's previous work, and it also provides a focal point for issues relating to the curriculum.

A supportive headteacher

Whilst it may be possible to develop design and technology successfully within a school where some parents or governors are not fully supportive, this is not the case if a headteacher is not supportive of the subject. Headteachers need to have an active involvement and encourage all involved, showing that they value the subject within the curriculum. Fullan (1982) includes this factor in his work on change and curriculum development and other research has indicated similar findings. The *Initiatives in Primary Science* report (ASE, 1988) highlighted the importance of the headteacher where successful change and curriculum development had occurred, whilst Benson and Johnsey

(1998) found similar patterns in their research project. Whilst financial support is useful, more important is the verbal support and obvious value which the head places on a subject. In one school that was fast developing an excellent programme, the headteacher, together with the staff, identified design and technology as a priority in the school development plan and the coordinator took part in a twenty-day in-service course. After the course, the whole school was involved in its dissemination; time was given to the coordinator to work alongside other members of staff and to develop appropriate documentation, and the coordinator was encouraged to be involved in work for publications and the Schools Curriculum and Assessment Authority (SCAA). Some school time was allocated for curriculum development and some came from the coordinator's own time. Standards rose in both pupil attainment and teaching. However, with the arrival of a new head, the development of design and technology within the school changed dramatically. The new incumbent did not understand the subject and had little interest in it. In staff meetings relating to curriculum development, she quickly identified other areas to focus on. Moreover, staff were not encouraged actively to share good practice in design and technology, displays were not commented upon and interest amongst staff and children waned. The original head moved on to a school in special measures where design and technology was identified as being weak. After two terms her enthusiasm for the value of the subject brought about marked positive changes in the attitudes of staff, parents, governors and children.

Whilst some curriculum development may take place without a supportive head, real success is achieved only if the leader identifies it as a school priority.

A school coordinator

Although less so than a supportive headteacher, a coordinator is also important in bringing about successful curriculum development. Since 1990 the identification of a subject coordinator for design and technology within primary schools has steadily risen according to the DATA survey (1998). In addition, there has been a marked decline in the coordination of the subject by headteachers or deputy headteachers. DATA saw this as an encouraging trend since headteachers and governors are now recognizing that the subject is important in its own right and needs a coordinator. Linked to this is the small increase in non-contact time that coordinators have been given since 1996. The identification of a person who can lead the curriculum development within a school is crucial to its success. Indeed Ive (1999) states that 'the presence of an effective subject co-ordinator in the school is the single factor that has lead to the greatest improvements in teaching in school' (p. 17).

Whilst the importance of the whole-school approach should not be forgotten, the role of the coordinator is crucial. Certainly it is important that the coordinator has a good knowledge and understanding of the subject, but at least of equal importance is the ability to enthuse and motivate others. A coordinator needs to be able to lead effective curriculum planning, to include progression and focused lesson planning, to provide guidance on the implementation of the subject in the classroom, to organize appropriate resources and to identify manageable assessment and recording methods. Part of the role includes monitoring and evaluating curriculum development in the school and, with the increase in non-contact time, this area of work should be undertaken by more coordinators. A supportive head and an effective coordinator can lead the curriculum development within the school, setting appropriate targets and supporting staff as they work to meet them.

Subject knowledge

It is hardly surprising that OFSTED (1996, 1998) has identified that one of the major weaknesses, particularly at Key Stage 2, is teachers' lack of subject knowledge. Where it is inadequate, standards are affected. Some teachers are unsure what to teach and will, if possible, only teach those areas with which they feel confident. This can lead to a programme which lacks both breadth and balance. No teacher experienced the subject in their own primary education and obviously it will be some time before sufficient numbers of newly qualified teachers with a subject specialization in design and technology are teaching in primary schools. The *Survey of Provision for Design and Technology in Schools, 1996/7* (DATA, 1998) has identified the professional development needs which schools have identified over the last four years. It is interesting to note that practical skills, planning and classroom management, and organization have always been high-priority areas, whereas skills and knowledge and understanding of, for example, mechanisms, structures and electronics are of lower priority. However, in the 1998 survey, whilst the relative importance of subject knowledge remains low, there has been a small increase in its importance over previous years. There are several reasons for this change. OFSTED reports may be having an effect on school priorities. Teachers may feel more confident about the organization and content of what they have to teach, and now have a clearer picture of what they need to know and understand. There are many more support materials which schools can use at INSET to help them to develop staff expertise. With a sound knowledge and understanding base, teachers can plan content more accurately, can deliver more effective teaching sessions and can assess more accurately, thus raising standards.

A national scheme of work

Whilst it was helpful to have a National Curriculum as a minimum entitlement for all children, it was not a scheme of work that identified the areas that should be taught in different years and when they might be taught. In 1990 there was little support for a national scheme of work from the government since it was felt that teachers might consider this prescriptive. A few LEAs produced materials, but many coordinators struggled to produce a meaningful scheme which covered all the programmes of study and provided clear progression, breadth and balance. As the National Curriculum was revised, teachers were constantly either anticipating change or trying to implement it. It was not until *Design and Technology: The New Requirements for Key Stages 1 and 2* (SCAA, 1995) and *Guidance Materials for Key Stages 1 and 2* (DATA, 1996) were published that schools had any support and guidance. Since 1996 there has been an improvement in the quality of planning (Ive, 1999). Whilst there is no data to identify how many guidance packs have been used in schools, over 15,000 have been purchased. QCA (1998b) offers additional support, and updates will ensure correspondence with the new National Curriculum for 2000. Already many schools are using the scheme. Some are using it as a check against a scheme which is already working well, whilst others have taken the whole scheme and made minor modifications to suit the needs of their children. There is now a flexible and manageable national scheme of work which schools can adapt to suit their needs.

Resources

Teachers need adequate, accessible and relevant resources in order to implement their schemes of work successfully. Certainly the amount of funding and the type of equipment which is needed within schools has changed over the last few years. Teachers' perceptions of the level of funding are indicated by the fact that over 50 per cent in DATA's 1996/7 survey (DATA, 1998) consider it to be adequate or generous. This has grown from 35 per cent in 1996. Of course it may mean that teachers have become accustomed to low levels of resourcing and expectations have therefore been lowered, or that indeed funding is now more appropriate to the needs of the subject. However there are still 35 per cent who consider it to be restricting learning, and 13 per cent who consider it to be curtailing elements of learning. It will be interesting to determine if the national literacy and numeracy initiatives have any perceived effect on the 1999 figures. Coordinators continue to carry the main responsibility for allocating capitation (67 per cent in 1998) whereas the class teacher's responsibility has fallen from 22 per cent in 1995 to 13 per cent in 1998. This could be related to the increase in the number of coordinators and the increased responsibility given to them for the provision of appropriate resources.

It will be of no surprise to the majority of primary teachers that additional funding supports the implementation of design and technology in many schools. The amount given by industry and commerce has remained fairly constant over the last four years, whereas specific funding from Parent Teacher Associations has decreased (DATA, 1998). Information was not available as to why this decrease has occurred. It could be that schools have secured a reasonable level of resources and have prioritized other subjects. Certainly literacy and numeracy initiatives have proved expensive and schools have needed to buy many additional resources in order to carry out the programmes effectively.

The changes in the type of resources that schools are buying do reflect the way in which curriculum development has moved forward. There has been a marked decline in the need for construction tools, equipment and benches as success, linked to these resources, has been achieved. From OFSTED report findings (1995, 1998), children's 'making' skills developed far more quickly than other aspects of the subject. In addition, the emphasis on professional development of teachers since 1996 has been far greater in practical skill development than in any other area.

Now that schools have increased their hardware, the focus of need has changed to software. This could be linked to the increasing emphasis on integrating ICT across the curriculum and, in particular, with design and technology. Indeed more ICT is identified in the revised programmes of study for design and technology in the National Curriculum for 2000 and teachers want to have appropriate software to enable them to carry out these new developments.

Adequate resources alone are insufficient to enable teachers to carry out quality design and technology activities. To ensure the best use of resources, the coordinator needs to determine a whole-school policy in relation to storage, ordering and maintaining supplies of consumables. Each school will make decisions relating to storage based on the physical layout of the school and the amount of space and quantity of resources available. Some schools have chosen to have a central resource base, others have appropriate resources based in each classroom, whilst others use both methods. To try to ensure that there is a supply of consumables, some coordinators set up systems whereby teachers forecast their needs at the beginning of a unit of work and indicate when any particular item is in short supply. Failure to have such systems in place can result in last-minute changes to activities or some valuable experiences being lost due to lack of appropriate resources.

Delivering teaching and learning

Having established long, medium and short-term plans, teachers need to determine how the content of the plans is to be delivered. It has never been the stated intention of government to dictate the way in which the National Curriculum should be delivered, although more recently methods for teaching the literacy and numeracy frameworks have been identified. From the DATA survey (DATA, 1998), it is apparent that primary schools have been moving away from a topic-based approach to teaching design and technology as a separate subject. However, the strategy that is used is less important than the quality of the delivery. Comments from teachers showed that whatever method was used, they felt that they had moved away from contrived integration which had never been of value to them or their children. It is not the case that meaningful links should not be made, even where design and technology is taught as a separate subject. From an examination of the programmes of study it is evident that strong links can be made with mathematics, science, art and ICT. Language is an integral part of all activities and there are opportunities to use all types of language in context (DATA, 1999). To ensure that the value of these links is realized, careful long, medium and short-term planning is essential. Coordinators of different subjects need to be aware of the links, and the areas to be studied need to be identified. Some knowledge and understanding may need to be introduced in one subject before being drawn on and applied in another. When planning literacy and numeracy sessions, schools are beginning to look carefully at ways in which they can incorporate design and technology contexts to make the sessions more meaningful. Examples include writing letters for information or to manufacturers, writing a report, writing notes and labelling drawings.

When planning individual activities, teachers have found the use of the three types of activity – investigative, disassembly and evaluative activities (IDEA); focused practical tasks (FPT); and design and make assignments (DMA) – to be invaluable aids to planning and an increased understanding of the processes involved in designing and making. OFSTED (1997) highlighted how this break down of activities has had a markedly positive effect on the way in which the subject is taught.

The way in which teachers have grouped children for design and technology has varied little over the last three years (DATA, 1998). Over 50 per cent are taught in small groups, 35 per cent as a whole class and a very small minority in extracted groups. Obviously factors such as resourcing and access to support staff play a part in determining how teachers organize their teaching, and best practice is seen where teachers have grouped the children to match the differing nature of the tasks and/or the differing abilities of the children. It is often assumed that children who are not in the top sets for English and mathematics will not be good at design and technology. Whilst there is little research evidence to refute this assumption, there is much anecdotal evidence. It is such an interesting issue that in a 1998 Channel 4 programme focusing on the transfer of children from Year 6 to Year 7, the producer chose to follow a child with learning difficulties. He was a high achiever in design and technology in Year 6 and enjoyed the subject. On transferring to the secondary school, it was his achievements in the subject that helped him to settle into school and not to feel a failure. Teachers should not make assumptions about children's abilities and, as in all subjects, they should consider differentiation when planning activities.

The future

The achievements of the last ten years in curriculum development for design and technology should be celebrated. However, there is no room for complacency by teachers and researchers. There is still a number of areas that must be improved in the very near future if design and technology is to continue to be valued as part of the primary curriculum. The development of teachers' subject knowledge is still a major issue. Despite the success of Grants for Education and Training courses (GEST) and other similar long award-bearing courses, there are still insufficient INSET opportunities to allow teachers to gain the knowledge and understanding that they need to be able to deliver the curriculum appropriately. Indeed Ive (1999) highlighted this area of concern and suggested that this should be a priority for the next few years. Children's designing skills are still not as well-developed as their making skills (OFSTED, 1998) and teachers need to develop strategies to support the development of these skills. Whilst the importance of ICT through design and technology has been recognized, more needs to be included in activities. Children need to use CD-ROMs and the Internet for their research; they need to use databases and spreadsheets during their designing; and they need to use control programmes more effectively in Key Stage 2. The success of INSET is proven (Ive, 1999). It is therefore crucial that INSET opportunities are increased so that all these areas for development can be addressed in a structured way. Individual schools need to review their present curricula in relation to the new National Curriculum 2000 (DfEE, 1999) to ensure that they have a scheme of work that offers breadth and balance and reflects the priorities of the school. Successful curriculum development is never complete; the cycle of consider, do and review is constant. Those educators who have realized the value of the subject and the contribution that it makes to the lives of young children will continue to ensure that the curriculum evolves to make it appropriate for education in the twenty-first century.

References

Aoki, T. (1984) 'Towards a reconceptualisation of curriculum implementation', in D. Hopkins and M. Wideen (eds) *Alternative Perspectives on School Improvement*. London: Falmer.

Association for Science Education (1988) *Initiatives in Primary Science*. London: ASE.

Benson, C. and Johnsey, R. (1998) 'The long term effects on schools and staff of in-service courses for teachers of primary design and technology', *Journal of Design and Technology*, **3**(1), 16–25.

Channel 4 (1998) *Bridging the Gap*.

DATA (1996) *Guidance materials for Key Stages 1 and 2*. Wellesbourne: DATA.

DATA (1997) *DATA's Initial Thoughts on the National Curriculum*. Wellesbourne: DATA.

DATA (1998) *Survey of Provision for Design and Technology in Schools 1996/7*. Wellesbourne: DATA.

DATA (1999) *Developing language through design and technology*. Wellesbourne: DATA.

DES (1990) *Technology in the National Curriculum*. London: HMSO.

DfE (1995) *Design and Technology in the National Curriculum*. London: HMSO.

DfEE (1999) *National Curriculum for 2000*. London: HMSO.

Fullan, M. (1982) *The Meaning of Education Change*. Ontario: Institute for Studies in Education Press.

Fullan, M. (1989) 'Planning, doing and coping with change', in F. Moon, P. Murphy, and J. Raynor (eds) *Policies for the Curriculum*. London: Hodder and Stoughton.

Ive, M. (1997) 'Primary design and technology in England – inspection evidence and "good practice"', in R. Ager and C. Benson (eds) *Proceedings of the First International Primary Design and Technology Conference: A Celebration of Good Practice*. Birmingham: Centre for Research in Primary Technology.

Ive, M. (1999) 'The state of primary design and technology education in England', in C. Benson and W. Till (eds) *Proceedings of the Second International Primary Design and Technology Conference: Quality in the Making*. Birmingham: Centre for Research in Primary Technology.

Marris, P. (1993) 'The management of change', in C. Mabey and B. Mayon-White (eds) *Managing Change*. Buckingham: Open University Press.

NCC (1990) *Non-Statutory Guidance: Design and Technology Capability*. York: National Curriculum Council.

OFSTED (1995) *Inspection Findings*. London: HMSO.

OFSTED (1996) *Subjects and Standards: Issues for School Development Arising from OFSTED Inspection Findings 1994–5*. London: HMSO.

OFSTED (1997) *Inspection Findings*. London: HMSO.

OFSTED (1998) *Inspection Findings*. London: HMSO.

QCA (1998a) *Maintaining Breadth and Balance*. London: Qualifications and Curriculum Authority.

QCA (1998b) *A Scheme of Work for Key Stages 1 and 2: Design and Technology*. London: Qualifications and Curriculum Authority.

Rudduck, J. (1989) 'Curriculum change: management of meaning?' in F. Moon, P. Murphy and J. Raynor (eds) *Policies for the Curriculum*. London: Hodder and Stoughton.

SCAA (1995) *Design and Technology: The New Requirements for Key Stages 1 and 2*. London: SCAA.

Webster, P. (1999) 'Raising the Status of Design and Technology through a Family Learning Focus', in C. Benson and W. Till (eds) *Proceedings of the Second International Primary Design and Technology Conference – Quality in the Making*. Birmingham: Centre for Research in Primary Technology.

Chapter 2

Identifying Designing and Making Skills and Making Cross-curricular Links in the Primary School

Rob Johnsey

Introduction

This chapter describes two linked research projects. The first used classroom observation to identify the skills used by primary school children as they designed and made simple products and led to valuable suggestions for improving classroom practice. It also provided the basis for exploring how other subjects such as science could be taught effectively by using design and technology as a vehicle for learning. This led to the second project in which trial materials were used in four primary schools giving rise to important ways to develop cross-curricular links with design and technology.

In order to know more about design and technology in the primary school there are a number of initial questions to ask. What is doing design and technology all about? What things do pupils do when they are successfully carrying out design and make tasks? Which skills do they already possess and what knowledge do they have to help them solve problems? We can then ask what skills, knowledge and under-standing pupils do not yet possess that would be helpful to them and what can be learnt in school to enhance their ability in designing and making. For answers we might look to successful designers, engineers or crafts persons or to the successful practice already taking place in schools.

Questions regarding how these answers might best be used to teach follow. How does the broad curriculum enhance learning in design and technology and vice versa? How can ideas learnt in one part of the curriculum be linked to design and technology?

The first project – Identifying the skills used by pupils as they design and make products

This project (Johnsey, 1995b, pp. 115–19), which spanned a period of three years, explored various ideas about how pupils or adults design and make products to solve problems. The project began with a survey of seventeen models of how people went about solving practical problems or carrying out design and make tasks. These turned out to be fairly similar and revealed a consensus of opinion as to what it was thought occurred during a design and make task (Johnsey, 1995a). Each

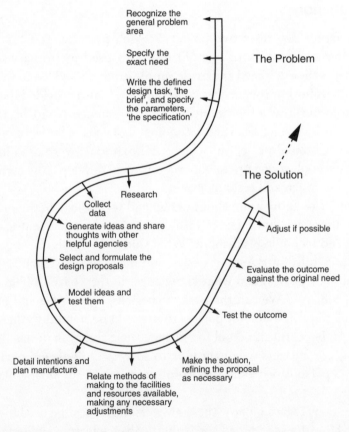

Figure 2.1 *The Department of Education and Science Design Loop (DES, 1987)*

model described a series of distinct skills which were combined in a variety of ways, often in a linear flow diagram. Figure 2.1 shows a typical example.

The research project described here challenged the accuracy of these simplistic flow charts by observing primary school pupils as they carried out design and make tasks.

Developing a coding system

A coding system which described the behaviour of pupils as they designed and made a simple product was developed in two ways. First, the descriptors used in the models described above were taken to form a list with common characteristics. Design skills such as *research and development* and *planning and organizing* were found to be common to many of the models. Second, a pilot study was carried out by making a video recording of a child as he carried out a design and make task. The list of descriptors was applied to the video recording and subsequently modified.

Eventually it was found possible to create a list of simple descriptors which could be applied to what a child was doing for every minute of a design task. An *off-task* descriptor was added later but was used very little, which suggests that when primary children are given a design task which lasts an hour or so they are very rarely found off-task. The following list of behavioural descriptors or *designing and making skills* emerged.

- *Investigating* the context for designing and making;
- *Identifying* the problem or the need;
- *Clarifying* the implications of the design task;
- *Specifying* the requirements of the outcome (setting the criteria by which the product will be judged);
- *Researching* the problem and its solutions;
- *Generating* ideas for a solution;
- *Modelling* a chosen solution;
- *Planning and organizing;*
- *Making* the product;
- *Evaluating* the product or partly made product or the procedures used; and
- *Off-task.*

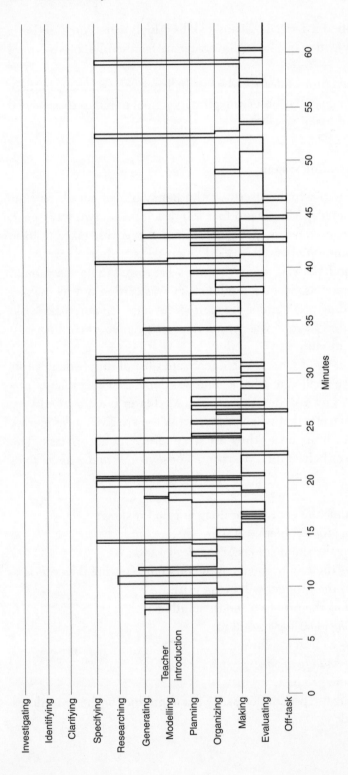

Figure 2.2 *A typical behavioural chart for a Year 5 child – Tariq*

These descriptors could be applied to a variety of case-study videos of primary school children as they worked in a classroom setting. The time spent by a child while displaying each of these behavioural characteristics was recorded and eventually mapped out on a behavioural chart which showed a 'snap shot' of the whole task. Eight of these 'snap shots' were gathered for children ranging from a four-year-old nursery child to a Year 5 pupil. Figure 2.2 shows a typical behavioural chart for a Year 5 child. The behavioural chart has a vertical axis representing the procedural skills. The horizontal axis shows the time in minutes after the beginning of the task. A few minutes were taken at the beginning for the teacher to introduce the task to the group. The horizontal lines on the chart show which skill was being displayed at any one moment during the activity. The vertical lines simply show the continuity from one skill to another.

Description of the activity

A small group of children worked in a classroom setting on an open-ended design task. This was to make a present with a moving part using the limited selection of materials available. Observations focused on one child, Tariq, who worked with a partner. Tariq and his partner decided early on to make a mobile but it became apparent that not all the details had been worked out in their minds. A number of decisions regarding the features of the model were made as it developed. This is shown by the number of *specifying* lines on the behavioural chart. The boys worked cooperatively together and discussed the solutions to many of the problems they encountered.

Initially the mobile consisted of two racing car cut-outs hanging from a single rod. Eventually the boys added a paper aeroplane which hung at the centre and was suitably decorated with red and yellow flames.

In contrast to most of the case-studies, Tariq and his partner decided to discuss their ideas and make a sketch of them before getting their equipment. This is shown on the behavioural chart in the early stages as *generating* and *modelling* ideas. The sketch enabled them to discuss details there and then. A survey of the materials available also helped them to decide what to make. The string and wooden rod were arranged to resemble a mobile before the boys settled down to draw and colour the cars. There was much interaction and agreement between the boys as they made the cars for the mobile.

Tariq decided to add a paper aeroplane to the central section of the mobile and proceeded to make it. The half-complete mobile was hung from the ceiling a number of times for evaluation and Tariq eventually made a hook for this purpose. In the time remaining the boys decorated the aeroplane which had become a dominant part of the model.

Interpreting the behavioural charts

The behavioural charts provide a rare chance to obtain an overview of a complete activity. However, they produce only a very 'coarse' picture of what went on. Much depended on the way in which the actions of the child were interpreted on video, although with practice this became reasonably consistent. Of course there were many variables which affected the shape of the chart such as the context of the design task, the particular child chosen to be observed, the setting in which the child worked and the effect of the observer.

With these constraints in mind it was decided not to expect too much from a comparison of the charts. For instance they were not detailed enough to show the difference in approach between a Year 2 child and a Year 5 child. Some observations were made in a classroom setting, others were made whilst a small group worked in a workroom. The nursery-aged child played alone for ten minutes with some building blocks while a Year 5 child made a Jack-in-a-box with a partner as a present for someone. The effects of these differences, while considerable, could not be detected in the behavioural charts.

What the charts could provide, however, was a set of characteristics common to each child and the way they worked. For instance each chart showed clearly that *making* was the dominant behaviour demonstrated and that *evaluating* was closely linked with each stage of making. A key feature of each chart was the untidy nature of designing and making, with many skills being used over and over again and in no particular order. Designing skills were often used late in each task and making skills were used early on. This is in contrast to the way in which designing and making is often described in neat flow diagrams in many texts.

The evidence from the behavioural charts suggests that when children are given a free hand to design and make, the making stimulates the designing as well as vice versa. It suggests that children do not plan everything at the beginning and then proceed but that planning runs in parallel with doing. Furthermore, it seems quite natural for children to change and add to the specifications they have for their product as they proceed. It is as though the half-completed product acts as a stimulus or modelling tool for new ideas. For primary-aged children who think mostly in concrete terms, this is, of course, not surprising.

Missing skills

The behavioural charts point to further lessons for the classroom. A number of skills seem under-represented and little used by the children. *Exploring* a context, *identifying* design and make tasks, and *clarifying* the task do not feature as part of each child's observed behaviour. This is largely because each task (with the exception of that carried out by the nursery child) was introduced by a teacher who by-passed the need for these skills. This was to save time and provide motivation for the tasks. In an educational setting, however, we might expect the teacher to promote the use of these skills when appropriate.

Design-related research is another skill which is also largely absent, possibly because of the time constraints and children's natural response to a practical task. This is not a skill that comes naturally to primary-aged children. Their response to a practical task is to use the knowledge they already possess to get on and solve the problem, especially when time is short. Research skills have to be taught and research opportunities and facilities have to be provided before children will use these and it is this theme which is examined in the second project described in this chapter.

Lessons learnt

The key lessons learnt from this research are:

- When primary-aged children are given freedom to design and make a product, what follows is a messy business which does not conform to a neat pattern or sequence of actions.
- Children do not naturally design something and then make it and finally evaluate it. These key skills tend to become dovetailed into one another throughout the task.
- Hands-on making is very important to children and may be of benefit in promoting the other procedural skills used in design and technology.

- The list of procedural skills developed for this project were found to work well in defining the skills used by children. While the way in which these were used was not always the same, they do sum up the skills that need to be taught.

Implications for the primary classroom

Teachers need to recognize that there are as many different ways of producing a design solution as there are design tasks. However, they need also to recognize that procedural skills and strategies are often common to a variety of design tasks, but that these may be used in different combinations and for different periods of time.

Having identified a procedural skill, teachers need to promote a variety of techniques for achieving the desired outcome. For instance, the process skill of *modelling* ought to help children to imagine what might be and should enable them to manipulate their ideas in model form. The 'model', however, need not be a design drawing. It might be a discussion, a series of hand gestures or a rapidly produced mock-up of the potential product.

The concept of a 'toolbox' which a pupil develops is helpful (Johnsey, 1998). For instance, if *modelling* is represented by one section in the toolbox then drawing, discussions, mock-ups or mental imaging become the individual tools which pupils can develop throughout their education. This clarifies what a teacher should teach and points to how a notion of progression might be developed. At the same time, however, pupils need opportunities to develop their ability to use the appropriate 'tools' in a variety of sequences within a variety of contexts.

Teachers can make children more aware of the procedures they are using as designers, thus focusing attention on activities which they do well and on those which require improvement. For instance, making clear to children the importance of on-going evaluation and how this is interspersed with making is likely to increase the quality of this skill in the learner.

When appropriate, children might be given practical tasks early in the design and make activity. Primary children appear to rely a great deal on a practical and physical interaction with the context within which they will design and make. The ability to handle materials and tools and investigate artefacts is a stimulus to other design and make skills such as specifying design outcomes and generating design ideas. The practical tasks need not involve making the final design product but could be closely associated with it.

At times the teacher can expect pupils to make choices which enhance their learning, as well as those which will lead to a well-designed and made product. For example, a child might choose to use wood strips and a junior hacksaw simply for the pleasure of manipulating a new material rather than producing an effective product. Teachers might arrange for children to become familiar with tools and materials so that their novelty does not detract from the design task in hand.

Teachers may expect children to spend a greater proportion of their time making but they should also identify when the making is, in fact, aiding their designing skills. Do not expect making to take place only after a complete design idea has been worked out. Making and designing work best hand in hand.

Teachers could use the idea of design-related research to educational advantage. Research activities can:

- stimulate new ideas for designed products;
- introduce new tool skills to the children;
- introduce new techniques to the children;
- introduce new design and technology knowledge (such as an understanding of a particular mechanism);
- introduce or reinforce knowledge from other areas of the curriculum.

Teachers could provide more time for certain process skills by structuring the timing of design and make tasks. For instance more time could be spent by pupils on evaluation skills if time for this were made available. Pupils might be encouraged to spend more time specifying the outcome of their task if this were promoted through discussion and/or written work and a specific time set aside for this to happen.

Teachers may plan work which encourages the development of a range of design and technology skills. The context of a design and make task will have an influence on the type of process skills used by the children. A short practical task such as recovering keys from a limited space is likely to encourage a lot of testing and analysis (*evaluating*). On the other hand, the production of a greetings card will encourage the use of *modelling* by sketching and a more subjective form of evaluation. The production of an electric-powered vehicle will require research into how electrical circuits, including switches and motors, are made. Schemes of work for design and technology are often structured to include opportunities for children to gain a breadth of *knowledge and understanding* in the subject. However, teachers should also choose design contexts carefully to provide experience in a balanced range of *design process skills*.

The second project – Teaching science with design and technology

A more recent curriculum development project (Johnsey, 1999, pp. 115–21) explored the concept of design-related research as a vehicle for learning. Science was chosen as the subject which might be taught through the use of a design and technology task, though this might equally have involved maths, art or another primary curriculum subject.

Design and technology is unique in that it is often dependent on *using* the knowledge and understanding learnt in other curriculum subjects. It is a subject in which pupils 'draw together and apply knowledge and understanding from other curriculum areas when forming practical solutions' (QCA/DfEE, 1999). This idea has been built into the rationale of the discipline ever since its inception as a National Curriculum subject, but it remains unclear how this mutually beneficial link can be made to work in the classroom. Focused practical tasks and evaluative and investigative activities have formed a part of teachers' vocabulary when planning units of work, but these have tended to refer only to design and technology knowledge and not that of other subjects.

This project sets out to teach science ideas as part of children's research for a design and technology task. It was important to achieve the learning objectives associated with both subjects and not allow one set to dominate the other. Furthermore, if children were introduced to the design task early in the project then they would be aware of the purpose of learning the science. They would not only reinforce their science understanding when it came to designing and making but the teacher would gain a valuable insight into how much the children had learnt.

How was each topic organized?

The project took place in two trial schools in the first instance, followed by a second phase in two more schools. Thus lessons learnt in the first

Table 2.1 *Organization of paired topics*

Science topic	Design and technology topic	Trial year group
Phase 1		
Pushes and pulls	Moving pictures	Year 1 (5–6-year-olds)
Changing sounds	Musical instruments	Year 5 (9–10-year-olds)
Phase 2		
Circuits and conductors	Torches	Year 3 (7–8-year-olds)
Friction	Moving toys	Year 5 (9–10-year-olds)

two schools could be applied in the second phase. Topics were chosen from the QCA schemes of work for Science and Design and Technology (QCA, 1998). The topics were linked in such a way that the design and make task would be enhanced by an understanding of the science. A number of schools were approached to explore whether the paired topics would fit in with their current scheme for that particular time of year. The topics are given in Table 2.1.

Case-study descriptions

The following accounts give a brief outline of each integrated topic.

Pushes and pulls and moving pictures

The children were in a mixed-ability class and were beginning a topic on *The Owl and the Pussy Cat*. The class worked for a two-hour period for five weeks. The teacher began by reading the poem and talking about the different kinds of animals in it and the movements these might make. The children described the parts of the animal that might move and described the kind of movement. They subsequently went on to relate these movements to themselves and their own muscles.

The children were introduced to the puppet task and asked what they would need to find out in order to complete the task. Only a few were able to provide ideas such as 'how to make it' and about the 'fluff', meaning the fur and feathers on the animals. They mentioned ways of making the movement – making 'slots', bending the card and making holes. One mentioned needing a knowledge of the materials that they would use.

In the second session the children linked their knowledge of movement with the pushes and pulls needed to produce this. They made a series of mechanisms involving pushes and pulls and wrote these words on their products. The children went on in the third session to discuss specifications for their puppet. A class list was made including: 'It should look fantastic'.

The children modelled ideas for their puppets by making scrap paper mock-ups and arranging these on their desks. They then went on to make the real thing using a card oval supplied for the body. Many were able to complete a working puppet, suitably decorated. Some children gave a short puppet show while the poem was read out. The children evaluated their puppets by completing an evaluation sheet with smiley faces.

Changing sounds and musical instruments

This trial was carried out with a Year 5 class of mixed-ability children. Previously they had not studied sound in science at Key Stage 2 nor made musical instruments although they had had regular music lessons supported by a well-equipped music room and music trolley. The class worked for a one-hour and then a one-and-a-half-hour session each week for four weeks and a single one-and-a-half-hour session in the final week.

The teacher began with a mystery sounds quiz in which the children tried to describe and identify some unusual sounds. This enabled the children to listen to sounds and build a vocabulary for describing them. In this same lesson the children were introduced to their design and make task – to make a musical instrument within a group that would be used to accompany a theme such as a television commercial. At this point the children were asked to identify the information they needed to complete the design task.

The children were asked to describe in a diagram how a person could hear the sound from a musical instrument of their choice. There followed a series of fairly formal science lessons in which the children explored sound with the purpose of preparing themselves for making instruments. These included work on vibrations, sound travelling in different media, the ear and investigating pitch. The children also designed and carried out an investigation in which they explored how to make sounds louder by using sound boxes.

Finally the children were asked to design and make an instrument from one of four basic categories: scrapers, beaters, strings or shakers. They drew the instrument they had chosen and went on to construct these in a single hour-and-a-half lesson. The project culminated in a short rehearsal and performance from each group of children. Individual children evaluated their own instruments in writing against a list of criteria they had devised for themselves earlier in the project.

Circuits and conductors with torches

This project was carried out with a Year 3 class who had no previous experiences with electrical circuits at school. The class worked for a two-hour period for five weeks.

The project began with a general discussion about things which used electricity. This was followed by a challenge in which the children were given a battery, length of wire and a bulb which they were asked to make light up.

The children were introduced to their task – to design and make a torch, light or lamp. There was a general discussion about the occasions on which a torch or lamp might be used and by whom. The children listed the kind of things they would need to find out to make their torch and then investigated a variety of battery-operated torches and lights.

The children went on to learn how to use battery holders, bulb holders and switches in a circuit. They learned how to make their own switches using aluminium foil, recorded some of their circuits in diagrams and learnt how to strip insulated wire and connect more than one battery.

The children wrote out their specifications for the torch they wanted to make and explored the materials available for construction before making drawings of the torch. They were asked to draw the wiring circuit in red felt pen on to their torch drawings. They went on to construct the torches and test them before evaluating the project as a whole class and individually on paper.

Friction with moving toys

This project was carried out with a Year 5 class in their classroom. The children began by looking at a variety of toys which moved in different ways. They were then introduced to their task – to make a toy in which

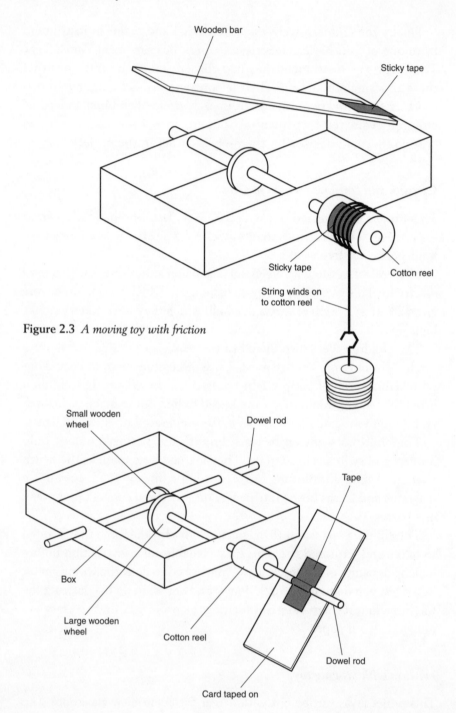

Figure 2.3 *A moving toy with friction*

Figure 2.4 *Friction between two wheels*

one thing bobbed up and down and another turned round. After discussing what the toy might represent the children wrote down the things they would need to find out.

The second part of the lesson introduced the children to an investigation into friction which would be of help in making the toy. Pairs of children were given a card box lid and a kit of parts which they made into a wheel and axle arrangement. A bar rested on the wheel causing friction to prevent the wheel turning. The children recorded the number of masses which were necessary to overcome the friction and start the wheel turning. They investigated the effect of different surfaces and a lubricant (Figure 2.3).

When it came to the design task the children wrote out their specifications for the toy and began to construct a wood strip frame to hold it. Much of the remaining time was spent on construction matters and getting the mechanisms to work. Eventually the children demonstrated their models to each other and wrote a short evaluation of their products by referring to their specification produced earlier.

Matching science content to that required for design and technology

The rationale for linking a subject such as science with design and technology is that the science learnt should be *useful* in developing a designed product. The application of knowledge in a new context helps to reinforce that knowledge and reveal how much has indeed been learnt. It became clear when planning each linked topic that the science knowledge in the scheme of work was often broader than that needed for the designing and making. For instance, the Year 1 children needed to 'observe and describe different ways of moving', whereas their simple puppets involved only a limited number of types of movement. The class studying friction needed to 'learn that friction can be useful' in a variety of everyday contexts, whereas the usefulness of friction in their model demonstrated only one specific example of this.

The design of a musical instrument did not require a knowledge of the working of the human ear and yet the science scheme demanded that this be included. Much of this 'extra science' was included as part of the learning programme but there was always a danger that the children would be side-tracked and lose sight of their practical task.

Different forms of science knowledge

An interesting feature of this project developed when an attempt was made to plan science activities which were of relevance to a practical design and make task. McCormick (1999) describes the different kinds of knowledge that a pupil might acquire in order to gain capability in design and technology. *Procedural knowledge* is concerned with how to go about solving problems, whereas *factual and conceptual knowledge* describes the ideas and information that might be required to complete the task successfully. He points out that this *conceptual knowledge* will often be presented in one form in a science lesson and yet be required in another form (*device knowledge*) in design and technology.

In the second phase of this project a conscious attempt was made to adapt the conventional science activities to suit the design task. The children making torches, for instance, were asked to make three different kinds of switch, each of which could easily be adapted for use in the torch. The children making the cam-driven toy were introduced to friction in a non-conventional way. They built a simple rig using a card box in which a wheel rotated and rubbed on a surface (wooden bar). The nature of this surface was changed by fixing different materials to it. The effect of using smooth surfaces such as plastic and lubricants such as washing-up liquid was investigated.

The use of this apparatus enabled the science learning objectives to be achieved while at the same time developing the children's device knowledge for their design and make task.

A second activity was developed using a similar rig (Figure 2.4) but this time enabling the children to explore how to increase friction between two wheels.

The conventional way of measuring friction in the primary classroom involves children pulling blocks along a table with a force meter to measure the friction produced. Such an approach would have been less appropriate in this instance.

Lessons learnt

Class teachers felt that the closeness in time between the science activities and designing and producing a product was of benefit to the children. A number of teachers described the increased motivation they had noticed as a result of their children knowing they were about to design and make a useful product. In all cases, science activities were followed within two or three weeks by designing and making and it was easy to remind the children of what they had already learnt.

In a number of instances the children continued to develop and reinforce their understanding of science ideas as they designed and made products. This was especially true of the group making torches since connecting circuits and avoiding short circuits and poor connections became part of the designing and making process. The children who made instruments were able to talk about changing the pitch and volume of sounds in their evaluations. This additional experience in developing science ideas through design and technology was often of a practical nature which was well suited to the children's learning needs in science.

Besides the chance to relearn ideas already encountered, many children were able to adapt what they had learnt to a new context and thus to expand their learning. Some children who had made an electrical switch in their science activity were able to make a new, more appropriate one for their torch. Those who had investigated using a hollow box to amplify sounds in a science experiment used this knowledge in making some of the musical instruments. Year 1 children who learnt about how pushes and pulls create different kinds of movement as part of their research were able to adapt this knowledge to make a head or tail move on their puppet.

One of the most apparent advantages of such an approach to teaching both science and design and technology was that the teacher could use the products made as an assessment tool for science. As children described their products it became very apparent how much science had been learnt. The girl who covered her bulb holder in silver foil as a decorative device had not appreciated the problems with short circuiting. The girl who glued smooth plastic to her cam was able to describe in detail how this reduced friction. Another who was asked to show where friction was occurring on her model merely pointed to the axle and clearly had not understood the concept in this particular context, despite detailed questioning by the teacher.

Summary

There are some useful conclusions which can be drawn from this curriculum development project:

- Careful planning and coordination are required to integrate science and design and technology in a meaningful way – but not all science can be taught in this way.
- Children do not easily transfer knowledge from one situation to another but the closeness in time within a single project helps this process.
- Children of all ages often need more help with their understanding of design and technology ideas such as construction techniques and mechanisms than they do with science ideas.
- It may be possible to develop design and make tasks which more readily use the science ideas that the children need to learn.
- Design and technology is a flexible subject which is largely to do with procedural knowledge which can be learnt within a wide range of contexts.
- In many instances the form of the science knowledge can be altered to suit the design and make task while still achieving the science learning objectives.

The idea that there are strong links between science and design and technology has been an assumption made for many years by educators working within both subjects. The assumption that science ideas, once learnt, can be automatically adapted by children for use in new contexts needs to be challenged. There is evidence to suggest there is considerable educational advantage in linking subjects such as science with design and technology in the way described in this chapter. However, the nature and form of the knowledge which is used in designing and making must be examined more closely. McCormick's concept of *'device knowledge'* as something which is more readily of use to pupils in their designing and making may require teachers to consider alternative ways of teaching science which, when appropriate, might then be more relevant to the real world.

References

DES (1987) *Craft, Design and Technology from 5 to 16*. London: HMSO.
Johnsey, R. (1995a) 'The design process – Does it exist? A critical review of published models for the design process in England and Wales', *The International Journal of Technology and Design Education*, **2**, 199–217.

Johnsey, R. (1995b) *An analysis of the procedures used by primary school children as they design and make*. MSc thesis, Warwick University.

Johnsey, R. (1998) *Exploring Primary Design and Technology*. London: Cassell.

Johnsey, R. (1999) 'An examination of a mode of curriculum delivery in which science is integrated with design and technology in the primary school', in P. H. Roberts and E. W. L. Norman (eds) *International Conference on Design and Technology Educational Research and Curriculum Development – IDATER 99*. Loughborough: Loughborough University, 115–21.

McCormick, R. (1999) 'Capability Lost and Found? – The Maurice Brown Memorial Lecture', *The Journal of Design and Technology Education*, **4**(1), 5–14.

QCA (1998a) *Design and Technology – A Scheme of Work for Key Stages 1 and 2*. London: Qualifications and Curriculum Authority.

QCA (1998b) *Science – A Scheme of Work for Key Stages 1 and 2*. London: Qualifications and Curriculum Authority.

QCA/DfEE (1999) *The Review of the National Curriculum in England – The Consultation Materials*. London: Qualifications and Curriculum Authority.

Supplementary reading

Anning, A. (1993) 'Technological capability in primary classrooms', in J. S. Smith (ed.), *IDATER 93 The International Conference on Design and Technology Educational Research and Curriculum Development*, Loughborough University of Technology, pp. 36–42.

Baynes, K. (1992) *Children Designing*. Loughborough University of Technology.

Bold, C. (1999) *Progression in Primary Design and Technology*. London: David Fulton.

DATA (1999) *Cross-Curricular Links Within the Primary Curriculum*. Wellesbourne: Design and Technology Association.

DfEE/QCA (1999) *The National Curriculum Handbook for Primary Teachers in England – Key Stages 1 and 2*. London: Department for Education and Employment/Qualifications and Curriculum Authority.

Hennessy, S. and McCormick, R. (1994) 'The General Problem-Solving Process in Technology Education – Myth or Reality?', in F. Banks, *Teaching Technology*. London: Routledge/The Open University.

Kimbell, R., Stables, K. and Green, R. (1996) *Understanding Practice in Design and Technology*. Buckingham: Open University Press.

Kimbell, R., Stables, K., Wheeler, T., Wosniak, A. and Kelly, V. (1991) *The Assessment of Performance in Design and Technology*. London: APU/SEAC.

QCA (1998) *Design and Technology – A Scheme of Work for Key Stages 1 and 2*. London: Qualifications and Curriculum Authority.

Ritchie, R. (1995) *Primary Design and Technology – A Process for Learning*. London: David Fulton.

SCAA (1995) *Key Stages 1 and 2 Design and Technology – The new requirements*. London: School Curriculum and Assessment Authority.

Chapter 3

How to Develop Problem Solving in Design and Technology

Peter Taylor

Setting the scene

Imagine a prospective design and technology teacher answering a question in an interview about the purpose of design and technology in schools. The response would often entail a defence based on its usefulness in preparing pupils for their place in an ever-changing technological society where transferable skills associated with problem solving are encouraged and valued. But how much do design and technology practitioners actually understand about problem solving within the context of teaching and learning design and technology?

Premise

While problem-solving activities have been central to the development of design and technology in schools, there appears to be a lack of sufficient understanding of the processes involved (Hennessy and McCormick, 1994; plus my own research into problem solving in design and technology[1]). This research indicates a lack of clear expectations about pupils' ability to work independently on problem solving, and about the ways in which problems could be set to match pupils' abilities.

Discussion

One of the major difficulties is the relationship between the development of design and technology as a 'subject' and problem solving as a 'concept'. Terms associated with 'designing' and 'problem solving' are often used in the same breath without sufficient regard for their meanings. Dodd (1978) considered that within the context of design and technology and the curriculum 'the problem-solving routine of the design-line offers opportunities for the complex development of understanding in a logical and purposeful way' (pp. 75–6). It can be seen that the development of the subject of design and technology has involved an almost symbiotic association between a school-based design process and problem solving. Indeed, McCade (1990) expressed concern that 'some use the terms "problem solving" and "design" inter-changeably. This approach is far too limiting' (p. 29).

Should problem solving be considered a sub-process of design, or vice versa? Research supports varying views. Within a study which set out to identify and describe problem-solving processes, thinking skills, teaching methods, and teaching styles typically used by 'expert' technology education teachers, DeLuca (1991) reported that respondents considered the design process to be just one of a number of activities within problem solving. However,

> . . .technology may be viewed as a way of meeting human needs by designing and making appropriate products. In some cases, technology is also viewed as a result of the problem solving process as the accumulated knowledge of processes and procedures becomes generally recognised and applied.
>
> (Blandow and Dyrenfurth, 1994, pp. 354–5)

There is considerable criticism of design processes and their utilization within design and technology. Roberts and Norman (1999) reflect on earlier work carried out by Roberts on design in general education where it was considered that design and designerly activity 'is a problem-centred activity (which is not to say that it is a problem-solving activity)', and that, 'it is distinguishable from other sorts of problem-solving activity by the fact that it is chiefly concerned with "ill-defined problems" (wicked problems)' (p. 125). Others have considered such problems as 'ill-defined' (Finke *et al.*, 1992), 'ill-structured' (Simon, 1973), or 'fuzzy' (Frederikson, 1984). Roberts and Norman (1999) subsequently acknowledge, however, that contemporary practice is based on a mixture of both ill-defined and well-defined problems, linked to a continuum with open-ended and constrained problems at the extremes. This can be seen to link to 'design and make tasks' and 'focused practical tasks'

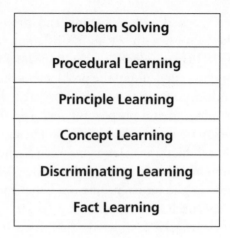

Figure 3.1 *Tufnell's hierarchy of modes of learning (1996, p. 6)*

(with 'investigative disassembly and evaluative activity' as the third strand) within the framework of the National Curriculum in England and Wales still operational at the end of the 1990s (DES/Welsh Office, 1995).

Some experienced practitioners and researchers have expressed concern about the over-emphasis of the term problem solving. For instance, Tufnell (1996) described how he disliked the term since the portrayal of design and technology as being concerned only with problems can be disheartening for pupils, and proposed it be replaced by 'exploiting opportunities' or 'searching for solutions'. However, he did consider that within the context of modes of learning, his personal version of a hierarchical structure (Figure 3.1) would feature problem solving as the most demanding.

Davies (1999) refers to earlier work associated with problem solving and creativity:

Design and technology capability is the National Curriculum defined term which locates the capacity to deal with design problems. Hilgard proposes two major approaches to addressing these through problem solving and creativity:

. . .the first of these relates problem solving to learning and thinking, as a type of higher mental process or 'cognitive' process. The second approach, supplementary rather than contradictory to the first, sees creative problem solving as a manifestation of personality and looks for social and motivational determinants instead of (or in addition to) purely cognitive ones[2].

(Davies, 1999, p. 103)

Research carried out by a team based at the Open University ('Problem Solving in Technology Education' – the PTSE Project) often used material derived from science and mathematics. Despite the observation that 'we are comfortable to think of creativity linked to the arts, but its association with technology is less usual' (Hill, 1998, p. 205), perhaps there is a case for balancing out such an approach with material derived from the realms of creativity. At the turn of the nineteenth century Herbart[3] identified 'five normal steps' of problem solving – preparation, presentation, association, generalization and application (Curtis and Boultwood, 1965; Shepard, 1990). Notions and theories of 'creativity' were subsequently developed which have often been represented in linear formats. Helmholtz developed a three-stage model at the beginning of the twentieth century based on 'saturation', 'incubation' and 'illumination' (Udall, 1994). Further models were subsequently presented, such as that by Wallas (1926) based on a four-stage model of 'preparation', 'incubation', 'illumination' and 'verification' (Branthwaite, 1986), and Getzels' 1960 five-stage model of 'insight', 'saturation', 'incubation', 'illumination' and 'verification' (Udall, 1994). Perhaps if the term creativity had been utilized to a greater extent in place of problem solving, subsequent discussion might have focused more on the relationship between creativity and design; and consequently we might have avoided the pitfalls associated with equating problem solving with designing. Is it the case that practitioners would more readily accept the concept of creativity within designing?

My own research confirms the opinion of Davies (1999) that 'Creativity is a little-used term in the field of design and technology education, but problem-solving isn't' (p. 103). Earlier models of design and technology, such as the design process proposed within the Design and Craft Education Project (Eggleston, 1976), indicate aspirations associated with creativity and the required balance between divergent and convergent thinking. Further research indicates a need for greater acknowledgement of creativity as an essential element in technological problem solving within the context of the varying effectiveness of different teaching styles (McCade, 1990). But can we actually teach creativity, particularly within an area which seems 'so steeped in convergent thought' (McCade, 1990, p. 34)? DeLuca (1991) develops the teaching theme further by using a hierarchical taxonomy through which it was found that the teaching methods associated with developing those cognitive skills linked with effective problem solving and high-level performance were seldom used. These teaching methods included seminar, scenario, contract, case-study, and panel discussion role play; and the corresponding teaching style was based on student development of goals and the means to reach them.

Ambiguities associated with problem solving in design and technology are unsurprising considering its nature. That there is considerable confusion associated with the teaching and learning of problem solving in design and technology is evident in the associated literature, as well as in opinions expressed by practitioners and pupils in schools. My own research involved the use of focus group interviews with 11- to 14-year-old pupils and their teachers in a series of schools and elicited responses on a number of major issues. Many differing opinions were expressed on the relationship between problem solving and design and technology: many saw it as being synonymous with the school-based design process, while others appreciated problem solving as a distinct approach in education alongside, and complementary to, design and technology. Most simply saw problem solving *as* the design process. However, according to Smith (1990),

> Procedures or 'strategies' – such as 'identify the nature of the problems', 'define and clarify essential elements and terms', 'judge and connect relevant information', or 'list possible alternative solutions' – are too obvious and too vague to be of any practical use. (p. 18)

McCade (1990) is more positive:

> Technology education changes problem solving from simply a means to an end in itself. Rather than use problem solving to produce a product, the product becomes one of many ways to teach problem solving. (p. 30)

Most teachers are concerned about pupils' ability to respond to open-ended design briefs and link this to their ability to solve problems. This applies both to higher-order thinking and to pupils' actual response to being 'taught' how to problem solve. Do we hope that repeated attempts to learn or to solve problems will automatically result in the improvement of general ability to solve problems (Segal and Chipman, 1985)? The development of higher cognitive skills that enable pupils to be independent learners and users of knowledge for creative problem solving has always been an important goal for educators. There is evidence, however, that explicit instruction in these skills is rare and that pupils' ability to problem solve is frequently inadequate (Segal and Chipman, 1985).

It is useful to remind ourselves that problem solving *is* a higher-level thinking skill (McCade, 1990). If we accept that this type of thinking involves analysis, synthesis and evaluation, and that it cannot occur without the appropriate supporting learning associated with knowledge, understanding and application, then we can relate this to Bloom's (1956) cognitive domain taxonomy, given at Figure 3.2 below.

It is maintained that 'Problem solving requires the student, guided by the teacher, to be able to function in all six levels' (Anderson, 1989, p. 3). That teachers and pupils have the additional pressure of manufacturing the developed solutions could indicate that we are just expecting too much of students. McCormick and Davidson (1996) found in the PTSE Project that the emphasis placed on making in design and technology can lead to neglect of problem solving skills. Superficial

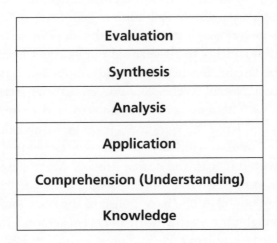

Figure 3.2 *Bloom's cognitive domain taxonomy (adapted from Bloom, 1956, p. 18)*

analyses have given the impression that much creativity and problem solving depends on the unlocking of hidden potential and the general tricks of thinking (Andre, 1989). However, effective problem solving in a specific area relies both on considerable specific knowledge and on general heuristics. This emphasizes the importance of the preparation stage of problem solving discussed by Wallas (1926). We must provide learners with an extensive knowledge base if they are to develop problem solving skills (Andre, 1989).

It may be useful for us to consider styles of learning to a greater extent within the context of this review. Included within this term are concepts such as the cognitive styles and learning performances of Riding and Cheema (1991) and Riding and Sadler-Smith (1992). Such material could be used to develop more effective methods of teaching and learning involving problem solving and based on the realization that individuals learn and process information in different ways, in contrast to the assumption in many design methodologies that individuals will learn equally well from the same basic teaching materials. Teachers (and teacher trainers) should be aware of individual differences in cognitive style and attempt to accommodate these into their instructional programmes.

Even if learning, thinking, and problem solving strategies exist, is it possible to teach them directly? Perhaps they must spontaneously emerge as a consequence of experience? Segal and Chipman (1985) maintain that it should be possible to select and design experience to speed up the process and that explicit instruction, linked to levels of cognitive activity, can also be helpful.

Part of my own research associated with groups of design and technology teachers and 11- to 14-year-old pupils asks whether problem solving can be taught. Teachers and pupils responded very differently to this question. Not all teachers considered that they actually taught problem solving within design and technology, and a number had not consciously considered this question. However, many believed that it can be taught. Those who did consider that they taught problem solving generally equated it with the design process. Many taught problem identification as opposed to problem solving. Only one teacher raised any discussion of cognition (in response to the question of teaching problem solving). One teacher, with an art background, doubted that pupils are able to problem solve and produce an 'artifact'.

The responses from the pupils did not always correspond to those of the teachers in their particular school. Some said that the teachers did not teach them how to solve problems, but this was not necessarily seen as a negative aspect. Those who considered that the teachers did teach them how to solve problems mentioned activities such as brainstorming, producing spider diagrams, providing information and giving demonstrations, and supplying part solutions or answers.

Conclusion

As teachers we should consider to a greater extent the benefits of an approach which encapsulates problem solving activities. However, there is a need to consider the appropriateness of teaching methods for different types of design and technology activity. Currently, a linear version of a design process dominates practical-based activity. There is a need to move away from 'six different ideas on a blank piece of paper' as a blanket approach to open-ended work. The starting point for curriculum planning should be the view that problem solving can be learned (Bransford and Stein, 1984). If we accept that problem solving exists as a developmental intellectual activity then we should consider teaching schemes in terms of a progressively more demanding process. It would follow that such a system should be considered initially and then appropriate projects and approaches to teaching would follow.

Pedagogical considerations

Considerations of such an approach should include the following:

- remember that problem solving involves high level thinking skills and is intellectually demanding;
- use a step-by-step approach to provide a structure enabling pupils to be creative;
- vary the systematic approaches in terms of the emphasis of that type of problem;
- teach appropriate sequence in the process but also consider that pupils (and teachers) have different preferred learning and thinking styles;
- consider the openness of the problem when setting activities – openness can affect the learning of technological concepts and processes;

- differentiate teaching and learning through the problem solving process. Show components of the big picture, break the problem down into manageable chunks (short-term objectives), and use scaffolding approaches;
- consider the pupils' learning as a form of apprenticeship and keep them informed of their progress;
- inform pupils of how you and others solve problems;
- have pupils think aloud – verbalization and reflection develop more effective problem solving abilities;
- have pupils work in pairs or small groups to a greater extent;
- reinforce questioning behaviour by positive responses phrased in terms of problem-solving strategies;
- provide situations for the transfer of learned problem solving skills – such a high-order skill requires that teachers facilitate links rather than relying on pupils to establish such links independently;
- use repetition to reinforce and practise problem solving skills – homework exercises could be based on different types of problem solving activity without the 'tyranny of the product outcomes' (McCormick and Davidson, 1996);
- justify the inclusion of any work and make problem solving an active process linked to real world events since a sense of purpose is of paramount importance;
- focus on process not on fact memorization;
- reinforce the importance of approximations and accuracy in terms of divergent/creative thinking and convergent/critical thinking.

The focus of this review of research has been on the nature of problem solving in design and technology and the extent to which problem solving can be learned. As such:

> The important thing about problem-solving is *not* that some people are better at it than others. Instead, the important point is that *problem-solving can be learned*. It frequently isn't learned because it isn't taught. In school, for example, we are generally taught *what* to think rather than *how* to think. This is not due to some great conspiracy to 'hide the secrets of thinking and problem-solving from the general public'. Instead, many teachers are simply unaware

of the basic processes of problem-solving *even though they may unconsciously use these processes themselves*. It therefore never occurs to them to make these processes explicit and to teach them in school.

(Bransford and Stein, 1984, p. 3)

Notes

1. Unpublished research completed as part of an MPhil: 'Problem-solving at Key Stage 3 in Design and Technology'. London: Middlesex University.
2. Hilgard, E. (1959) 'Creativity and its cultivation', in H. Anderson (ed.) *Creativity and Problem Solving*. Haarer Professional and Technical Library.
3. Herbart, J. (1892) *Science of Education*. Boston, MA: D.C. Heath.

References

Anderson, L. (1989) 'Problem solving in technology education', *The Technology Teacher*, **49**(1), 3–7.

Andre, T. (1989) 'Problem solving and education', in P. Murphy and B. Moon (eds) *Developments in Learning and Assessment*. London: Hodder and Stoughton.

Blandow, D. and Dyrenfurth, M. (eds) (1994) *Technology Education in School and Industry: Emerging didactics for human resource development*. Berlin: Springer-Verlag.

Bloom, B. (ed.) (1956) *Taxonomy of Educational Objectives: Book 1. Cognitive Domain*. New York: Longman (David McCay).

Bransford, J. and Stein, B. (1984) *The Ideal Problem Solver*. San Francisco: Freeman.

Branthwaite, A. (1986) 'Creativity and cognitive skills', in A. Gellatly (ed.) *The Skilful Mind: An introduction to Cognitive Psychology*. Milton Keynes: Open University Press.

Curtis, S. and Boultwood, M. (1965) *A Short History of Educational Ideas* (4th edition). London: University Tutorial Press.

Davies, T. (1999) 'Taking risks as a feature in the teaching and learning of design and technology', *Journal of Design and Technology Education*, **4**(2), 101–8.

DES/Welsh Office (1995) *National Curriculum Design and Technology Statutory Order*. London: HMSO.

DeLuca, V. (1991) 'Implementing technology education problem-solving activities', in *Journal of Technology Education*, **2**(2), 5–15.

Dodd, T. (1978) *Design and Technology in the School Curriculum*. London: Hodder and Stoughton.

Eggleston, J. (1976) *Developments in Design Education*. London: Open Books.

Finke, R., Ward, T. and Smith, S. (1992) *Creative Cognition: Theory, Research and Applications*. Cambridge, MA: MIT Press.

Frederikson, N. (1984) 'Implications of cognitive theory for instruction in problem solving', *Review of Educational Research*, **54**(3), 363–407.

Hennessy, S. and McCormick, R. (1994) 'The General Problem-Solving Process in Technology Education – Myth or Reality?', in F. Banks (ed.) *Teaching Technology*. London: Routledge/The Open University.

Hill, A. (1998) 'Problem solving in real-life contexts: an alternative for design and technology education', *International Journal of Technology and Design Education*, 8(3), 203–20.

McCade, J. (1990) 'Problem solving: much more than just design', *Journal of Technology Education*, **2**(1), 28–42.

McCormick, R. and Davidson, M. (1996) 'Problem solving and the tyranny of product outcomes', in *Journal of Design and Technology Education*, **1**(3), 230–41.

Riding, R. and Cheema, I. (1991) 'Cognitive styles: an overview and integration', *Educational Psychology*, **11**, 193–215.

Riding, R. and Sadler-Smith, E. (1992) 'Types of instructional material, cognitive style and learning performance', *Educational Studies*, **18**(3), 323–39.

Roberts, P. and Norman, E. (1999) 'Models of design and technology and their significance for research and curriculum development', *Journal of Design and Technology Education*, **4**(2), 124–31.

Segal, J. and Chipman, S. (eds) (1985) *Thinking and Learning Skills, Volume 1: Relating Instruction to Research*. Hillsdale, NJ: Lawrence Erlbaum.

Shepard, T. (1990) *Education by Design*. Cheltenham: Stanley Thornes.

Simon, H. (1973) 'The structure of ill-structured problems', *Artificial Intelligence*, **4**, 181–201.

Smith, F. (1990) *To Think*. New York: Teachers College Press.

Tufnell, R. (1996) *Design and Technology: Practically Essential* (Inaugural Lecture, Middlesex University, 26 November 1996).

Udall, N. (1994) '*The Mobius Ring*: a model for creativity', *Co-design*, **1**(1), 26–30.

Wallas, G. (1926) *The Art of Thought*. New York: Harcourt Brace Jovanovich.

Chapter 4

Researching the Art of Good Teaching in Design and Technology

George Shield

Introduction

Changes in the management and structure of the design and technology curriculum over the last decade, together with new initiatives in the training of teachers, and the decimation of Her Majesty's Inspectors of Schools (HMI) and local education authority advisory services have caused the basis of the subject to be questioned. The underlying philosophies are being lost and it is alleged that the subject area has lost its sense of direction (Smithers and Robinson, 1992).

Yet the basis of much of the work in design and technology is more relevant now than it has ever been: life skills such as problem solving and thinking skills, the ability to work in teams, the fostering of self-confidence and similar ephemeral qualities are today heralded as essential for modern life. This concern over the technology curriculum is not restricted to the UK. Similar reservations are being expressed in countries as diverse as the USA and Botswana, Japan and Sweden (Ginner, 1995; Botswana Ministry of Education, 1996; Dugger and Newberry, 1997; Yamazaki, 1999) and we must learn from colleagues elsewhere in the world as well as from informed debate and research in the UK.

This research is a contribution to the debate on the development of the design and technology curriculum by illustrating how the practical concerns of teachers, such as the resource environment and management of the learning experience, have an essential contribution to make in any developments that should result. Changes should not take place based solely upon concerns emanating from the needs of the economy or political orthodoxy.

Methodology

This piece of research was designed to investigate how good teachers of technology carry out their task and the possible implications this may have for other practitioners. The research was based upon an assumption that curriculum models devised by experts and educational philosophers in isolation from the practice of technology education must be revised in the light of professional practice. What is actually going on in the classroom is a very important pointer to what and how children learn, and must be considered before wholesale curriculum revisions are implemented.

The work of technology teachers in eight secondary schools in the north-east of England was studied. Reasons for using this research strategy are similar to those of other researchers into the practice of teachers:

- expert teachers reflect their experience in their classroom performance;
- in presenting a holistic picture, three types of activity should be considered; instructional, management and social extending over the preactive, interactive and reflective phases of teaching (Silberstein and Tamir, 1991, p. 166).

In selecting schools I fell back upon established practice to decide upon the criteria to be used. Silberstein and Tamir (1991, p. 167) made two suggestions to overcome this type of difficulty:

- subjective criteria such as the evaluative judgement of significant others, and
- objective criteria such as continuous and consistently high achievement of the pupils.

With these in mind, I used subjective criteria (e.g. advice from 'experts' in the field) and, wishing to be as rigorous as possible, objective criteria such as examination results. Other considerations included a sample of schools from a range of local education authorities as well as a range of different organizational structures. The schools also volunteered to help with the work, after my initial approach, indicating a self-confidence in their capability.

The instruments used to gather data included interviewing, observation of the teacher in action, the use of a field diary to record anything that may have had a bearing on the work of the school, and the scrutiny of other sources of information such as departmental handbooks, teachers' handouts and examination and test papers.

In the interviews the questions were explored through discussion of key themes using an approach termed the conversational interview. This was used mainly to go beyond established or official views.

Data analysis

When working with data that can be translated into numbers there are various accepted statistical packages that will analyse the raw data and come up with a range of information. These established methods give confidence in at least two ways. The assurance that others have used similar methods and have received little or no criticism enables you to present your findings with the weight of established 'case law' behind you. Using numbers invokes a feeling of objectivity that is often difficult to establish from apparently subjective opinions obtained from data such as observations or interviews.

Whilst these apparent advantages are attractive (and often seductive) no such authority can be placed upon qualitative methods of interpreting data. This, however, can also be seen as an advantage. If researchers want to devise new analytic tools to interpret data they are free to do so. The onus would be on establishing the reliability and validity of the strategies employed so that the work can be checked and findings verified. The major initial task was to identify common elements or themes, which were then scrutinized to develop the central themes or underlying principles linked to the work. The fundamental problem was the difficult task of avoiding identifying simplistic or superficial incidents and to achieve a more basic underlying interpretative analysis. There is always the danger of the researcher reading into apparently significant occurrences more than is there, or missing critical aspects. For example, simply counting the number of times a topic came up in conversation or during interviews with staff may be interpreted as showing that the subject is highly significant. But it may only be 'topical' rather than 'fundamental'.

Therefore, the analysis process was systematic and comprehensive, but not rigid. It was ongoing, and as it developed it informed later stages so that the researcher became more skilled and gained greater insights into the activities under observation.

A major initial difficulty lies in defining or identifying the research question. One way forward is to realize that the questions that identify

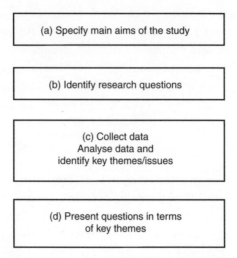

Figure 4.1 *Initial questions (Kyriacou, 1992)*

good practice cannot be identified initially, i.e. the hypothesis cannot be formulated in advance, and strategies must be developed to aid the initial questioning that takes place. This approach is illustrated in Figure 4.1.

Research may have a theme that will provide a focus (a), for example the researcher may have a general interest in process methodology but be unable to formulate a precise hypothesis. This interest may then lead to questions which are of a general nature (b), such as *How does technology fit into the school structure? How do the teachers conduct their classes? How do the children learn?* In (c) the collected data is then scrutinized to see if patterns of behaviour or particular issues emerge. The results of this analysis (d) both form the specific questions and provide a structure for insights into the practice of that teacher or institution.

In technology education the search for data to form the basis of informed comment is complicated by the nature of the learning process that takes place in the technology lesson. The range of concepts covered is extensive and the learning activity itself is based predominantly on a range of practical activities.

The basic tools of the work include interviewing, observation of the teacher in action, the use of a diary to record any occurrences that may have a bearing on the work of the school, available documentation and the scrutiny of other available sources of information. One of the problems is that of establishing the realities of the situation. The true 'facts' are difficult to identify and clarify through a questionnaire or structured

Key themes and issues

1.0 The place of technology within the school

2.0 The teaching process

3.0 What type of learning takes place?

4.0 Rhetoric *v* Reality

5.0 Intellectual involvement

Figure 4.2 *Initial topics*

interview. The tendency to produce the 'correct' answer or the response that pleases the researcher is strong. Each aspect of the work demands time to explore and try to reveal the meanings behind responses.

In this work the initial range of topics was compiled from data that emerged from various sources such as informal discussions with teachers, conference papers, and journal articles following the use of the strategy outlined in Figure 4.2.

This list was then broken down and subdivided into topics that were important for the study so that a chart could be completed (Figure 4.3). These topics emerged from a range of data. The data were fluid and constantly amended in the light of new insights being gained.

The headings for the classification were not fixed, neither are they in any order of priority. They merely appeared to be significant in terms of the bank of information that had been collected. This significance could, for example, lie in the regularity with which a particular topic occurred, or even the fact that it was very important in one school but not mentioned elsewhere. Also, it will be seen that some of the data can be classified under more than one heading (Tesch, 1990).

Once this initial categorization had taken place, the evidence could be extended to inform conclusions that helped the decision making process.

This evidence appeared as follows:

A. 1.1 (From department handbook) The Technology area consists of independent departments representing the traditional areas of CDT, H.E., Art, Business Education and Information Technology. The work of these departments, for the purpose of the National Curriculum, is co-ordinated by the head of CDT who has this management responsibility delegated to him by the Head Teacher.

A. 1.1 (Interview with head of dept) This approach is designed to retain the autonomy of the school's traditional subject areas which are recognized to have knowledge bases which are distinct but which are also seen to have elements, particularly in terms of methodology, in common. The majority of these common elements have been identified to meet the requirements of the National Curriculum.

B. 1.1.1 (From field notes) Teacher T4 is the head of faculty. He had also entered teaching as a mature student having been working in an accounts department for a number of years. His initial teacher training was as a specialist craft teacher and all of his subsequent expertise has been acquired 'in-service'.

B. 1.1.2 (From interview with class teacher) Other points which emerged from this interview included the difficulties in reconciling the range of expertise required by the National Curriculum with expertise available. Whilst the 'carousel' system was thought to have advantages from this point of view, it was realized that a drawback was the difficulty in ensuring progression. In an ideal situation it was thought that a centralized facility may be of help in delivering the 'integrated' approach required.

D. 1.1.2 (From school brochure) The faculty of Technology includes the departments of CDT and Home Economics. Art is not part of this organization being seen to be part of an arts faculty but also as having a considerable part to play in its own right.

What this and large amounts of similar data revealed was that whilst the official line of the research sample of schools was that the schools were divided into faculties and all had technology coordinators, they were in fact functioning as departments and finding it extremely difficult to implement the National Curriculum along recommended lines (NCC, 1993). This information may not be apparent from a straightforward analysis of a questionnaire.

The case-studies

Teaching techniques

In examining the practice of teaching, different techniques were used. In some cases the movement of the teacher around the workshop was analysed to discover the number and type of interactions that took place between the teacher and the taught, and these movements were plotted on a chart. In the example shown (Figure 4.4) the teacher was working with a group of 13-year-old children who were constructing a toy which has to have movement built into it. The work was based on mechanisms and included levers, cams and gears.

From this and other examples it was shown that the teachers work extremely hard physically and intellectually. They were constantly moving around the room interacting with each child, in one case on demand. With another teacher the movement was more systematic but again, as the lesson developed, on demand.

The layout of the room dictates teachers' movements and consequently their ability to interact with the whole range of children. Due to the individual nature of the work they are also having to deal with a considerable range of problems that are intellectually demanding. What is perhaps more interesting is the nature of the interaction that is taking place, i.e. just what are the teacher and taught talking about?

To look at this, the teachers were fitted with a micro tape recorder for a whole lesson and the recording analysed. It soon became apparent that a considerable amount of time was spent dealing with comparatively mundane, though essential, tasks such as pointing out where to find materials and preparing materials on machines that the children were not equipped to use. The following interchange between a teacher and his pupil is typical (Shield, 1992):

P   Sir, where's my folder?
T   Everybody's work is in there.
P   Sir, where's the numbers for the clock?
T   In here.
P   Paper.
T   What colour?
P   What colour is there?
T   There'll be some green and some blue. Some red, some grey, some black.
P   Sir, can I have some red?
T   Yes. Go down to my office – you know, at the end of the corridor. On the filing cabinet. O.K. Green and blue on the filing cabinet and in room . . . , which is in the corridor in the brown drawing cabinet – in the third drawer up from the bottom. Some large sheets of sugar paper, that's where you'll find the red.
P   Sir, where will I get . . . for that.

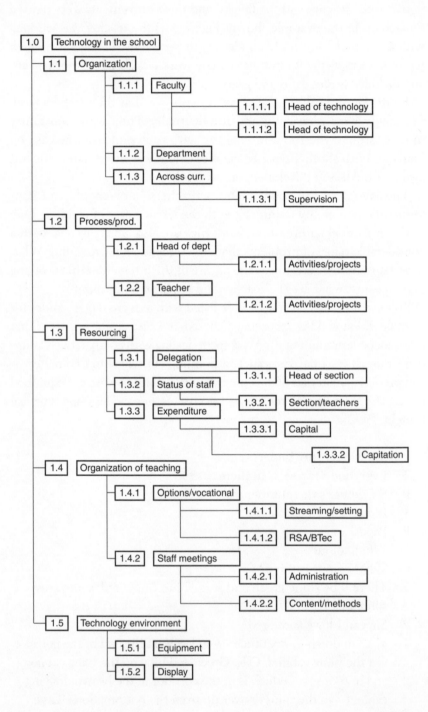

Figure 4.3 *Categorizing topics*

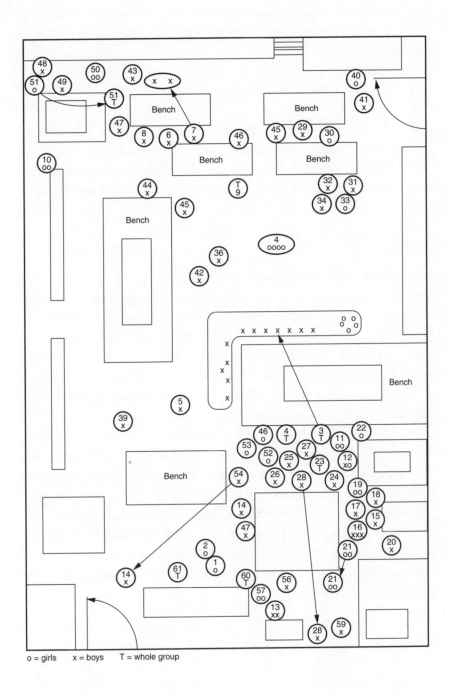

Figure 4.4 *A workshop environment*

In these following two examples however, it can be seen that not all teachers interact in the same way. Mr John was more concerned with 'thinking' skills:

T   Right then Edward, tell us how we got on with this.

P   . . .

T   Do you think that's going to work? That's going to have to be a little bit wider. Do you know what . . . do you know what perhaps we should do? I'm not sure about that dovetail there. I'm not so sure that it should be a straight spigot going out. Either that or you're going to have to open this space perhaps a little bit.

(Shield, 1992, p. 47)

He used this approach through most of the lesson. Constantly moving around advising on design principles, making techniques and, very often, economy in the use of materials. Mr Simon, however, from a different school, was far more concerned with getting the facts across. In a detailed analysis of a period of one hour during one of his lessons he asked 28 open questions and 52 closed. Closed questions are defined as those requiring a factual answer, whilst the open questions invited the students to think and contribute to the discussion.

During this session the children were engaged in individual work. Interestingly, the majority of the questions were closed in order to elicit problems encountered by the children. He would then proffer advice or demonstrate some technique or process. The open-ended questions were used to draw from the children their thinking on a particular topic. Again, this was then used to extend the children's knowledge base.

This teacher was particularly prolific in giving information to the children and the type of advice and the number of times it was given during one lesson was noted:

Information	
Process	6
Content	60
Facilitate	35
General	6
Admin. Instructions	14

In perhaps the most important case, a tape recorder was placed near a work station whilst a group of children were designing a mechanism for a robotic arm (they were working on an adaptation of a bicycle brake mechanism). Some interesting insights into group dynamics and the process the children were going through were revealed.

P1 Mine'll work won't it?

P2 Should do.

P1 Ya naa the bit that gan's like that and the bit that taks the loop, and the wire gaans in and oot there. That'll be really tight an all.

P2 Small and tighter. Normally you pull the wire longer and . . . where's the book?

P1 I think that'll get smaller . . . but the wire'll get bigger.

LATER

T   How much was it?

P3 We'll measure the square right? Then we'll know the distance we'll take for the square you put it in. You measure the distance what'll be when you put it upside down.

Here the children are problem solving by discussing designs amongst themselves. They have recognized the need to use reference material and are engaged in mathematical concepts.

Student learning

In another case a concept mapping technique was used to try to find out what the children had learnt from one teacher about mechanisms. Time was spent explaining what a concept was and the purpose of the concept map before the group was set to work. The responses were classified according to boys and girls and the concepts were divided into three categories:

1. The scientific/technological concepts of mechanisms, i.e. responses which referred to levers, cams, linkages, etc. These could be said to reflect the content or cognitive learning which took place during the lesson.

2. Concepts which mentioned objects such as machines, i.e. cars, drills and computers. These could be said to reflect a lay person's view of mechanisms.
3. Concepts such as energy and efficiency. These could be said to indicate a deeper understanding of the more abstract facets of the topic.

When the results of this experiment were reviewed (see Figure 4.5) it was unsurprising to see that the largest response was in the area I have termed the 'lay view', with 63 per cent of the girls' responses and 55 per cent of the boys' recorded here. The overall figure was 57 per cent. This result would suggest that the children had a large residual background knowledge of technology that could have been acquired through learning experiences outside the technology class as well as part of a structured learning programme. This knowledge could well (and probably did) arise from experiences that were not part of a formal learning activity.

In another case analysis centred on the internal test papers set. At this school the importance of subject knowledge and conceptual understanding was reinforced through the use of a formally structured and administered paper and pen test that was used to evaluate the knowledge gained and to supplement the subjective evaluation of the project itself. The test paper included questions designed to test high-order activities such as evaluation, together with the recall of factual information. The knowledge base of the children was tested through 70 per cent of the questions with the remainder devoted to reasoning activities. This highly factual approach to teaching can be seen at work in the example in Figure 4.6 of a design brief which was set for the children in the same school.

The example shows a highly prescriptive approach to teaching a particular electronic circuit with a thin veneer of designing. The children, in effect, ended up 'designing' a switch.

Validity of the research

One of the most common criticisms levelled at research of this nature is the apparent lack of objectivity and validity in the findings obtained. This is a limitation that has to be recognized at the outset of the research and attempts must be made at all times to eliminate researcher bias and methodological shortcomings. All research is subjective to some degree

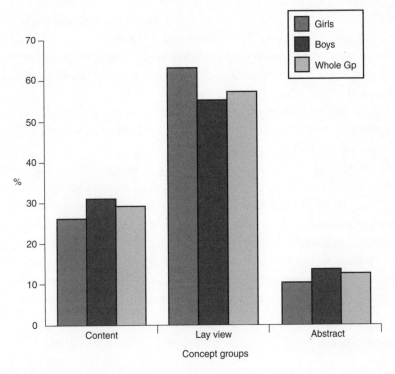

Figure 4.5 *Technological concepts (Shield, 1992)*

Design Brief   *Year 8 Design and Technology*

A manufacturing firm has identified a market for electronic games which rely on the manual dexterity (Hand skill) of the players.

Design and make a prototype for a new game.

Specification

The game must:
1) Use a 9v battery
2) Use a light emitting diode (LED)
3) Use a resistor (330 ohms)
4) Use a buzzer
5) Be made from available materials.

Figure 4.6 *Extract from design brief set for Year 8 children in school H*

and this is reflected in the questions asked and the conclusions reached. For example Scarth and Hammersley (1986) recognize the conflict between what the intentions of a teacher are in setting a task or carrying out a particular course of action, and the researcher's interpretation of this action.

To overcome this drawback discussions with participants in the research can take place, and the resulting opinions can be subjected to an examination by critical friends.

There should also be thorough use of a wide range of instruments. Field notes should be kept, interviews taped. Lessons can be recorded to keep an accurate account of teacher–pupil interaction and photographs taken (Dieckman, 1993). Other records such as pupil work sheets and school documentation should also be available for scrutiny. It is in these terms that the value of the research is recognized. The validity of the work is interpreted as 'the correspondence of knowledge claims to the reality investigated' (Hammersley, 1992. p. 196).

Conclusions

Whilst most of the teachers involved in this study were not only very aware of the nature of problem solving models or algorithms but also employed them consistently in their work with their students, they often supplemented such approaches with very traditional rote learning and didactic teaching strategies. The tendency to 'work to the exam' was very marked. Teachers took great pains to emphasize the need to provide 'evidence' of activities, such as producing a range of solutions to their brief or their research, whilst often not spending the time necessary to improve these very same activities in practice. In other words the 'rhetoric' became the 'reality'. If students could show that they had five examples of a solution to a brief or product in their 'design folder', it was assumed that these alternatives had been analysed meaningfully and appropriate conclusions drawn. In fact they were often window dressing for the sake of the examination.

The technology teachers were highly active. The complexity of the interaction between teacher and learner, and also the unpredictability of the outcomes of learning through a process model, were seen to put considerable demands on their stamina and versatility. To be successful the teachers needed to be able to overcome the difficulty of preparing for the unpredictable. The solution to this problem appeared to be achieved through a confidence in their technical understanding and at the same time an ability to anticipate (or even plot) the problems students were likely to meet. Through these abilities and strategies the teacher focuses the attention of the student upon relevant concepts that can be modified and then internalized.

Making individual project work effective as a means of delivering technological concepts was seen to be difficult. When the children were working on individualized programmes it was very difficult to ensure that content delivered through whole-group teaching had immediate relevance to the work of the individual student. Teachers overcame this in two ways – simply to severely limit the brief, and simply to repeat the content to each child, or small group of children, when appropriate. These strategies either compromise the ideal of problem solving or are highly inefficient in using the teacher's time.

If curriculum objectives that stress the acquisition of higher-order technological understanding are to be achieved, strategies must be devised which recognize the limitations of teaching, learning and assessment methods, the structures of organizations and the limitations of resources, both human and material, needed to implement them. Curriculum innovation by diktat is not only ineffective but may also in extreme cases be harmful. The alternative scenario appears to be one in which teachers rely on their craft skills to achieve a shallow success which is attractive to both their pupils and those charged with evaluating performance. This short termism fails to serve the subject area, society at large or, most importantly, the children.

Conclusions that can be drawn from this work could be far-reaching, particularly when they are linked to recent thought on some of the underlying assumptions in the National Curriculum. For example if the 'process' of problem solving that is the driving force behind much of our current philosophy is being circumvented by teachers in their search for 'effective' teaching strategies and examination success, should this fact not be recognized? If it is necessary to 'break the rules' for success, should the rules not be changed?

Furthermore, there is increasing evidence that such concepts as generalized problem solving skills are questionable. That learning and problem solving is 'context-based' and ought to be recognized as such. This 'context' is not only related to the issues to be addressed but also, within the school or college, to the total learning environment. In physical terms, this is not necessarily an excessively 'neat' atmosphere but one that is stimulating, orderly and provides easy access to learning materials. The display of visual and attractive material serves not only as a decorative feature and motivational stimulus to pupils but also as a guide to solutions that had been used previously.

In departmental management terms care should be taken to encourage close teamwork among colleagues. This is important to ensure progression through the curriculum and also to guarantee that the philosophical underpinnings of the teaching and learning strategies employed by the department are interpreted in a similar fashion. 'Management' should be an essential element in in-service programmes for design and technology teachers.

Where does our work go in the twenty-first century? I suspect that the first thing that we will not be able to escape from is the way in which information and communication technologies (ICT) are beginning to dominate our way of life and increasingly in the future our education system. The changes will be on two fronts. First will be the more usual recognizable task of keeping up to date with emerging technologies and trying to transmit that knowledge to our pupils. Second and more important will be understanding how we can use these to aid the learning process.

It is obvious that ICT can be used to aid learning in technology education. As well as the retrieval and manipulation of information necessary to inform designing, there are also increasingly sophisticated packages designed to aid the creative act itself. With the advent of advanced technologies this whole process is telescoped and results are gained more quickly and more accurately. However, the real breakthrough will occur when truly interactive packages that provide rich learning environments, recognize the student's learning style and also take into account complex learning theories, are available in a form that makes them readily available to teachers. Nevertheless, this can only ever be a partial solution since technological capability should, in most cases, come from the development of tangible solutions to problems and involve more than a virtual product.

The use of ICT will always be only one strategy in the range of resources available for the teacher to use; it is after all the creative act in a range of materials that embodies the true educational value of work. Creativity within ICT media is an essential and worthwhile activity in its own right but this does not justify its being the sole, or even a major, approach to an education through technology. Design skills and the enhancement of conceptual understanding whilst essential must be accompanied by the ability to translate these understandings into tangible solutions.

References

Botswana Ministry of Education (1996) *Design and Technology Three-Year Junior Certificate Programme*. Gaborone, Botswana: Botswana Ministry of Education.

Dieckman, E. A. (1993) 'A procedural check for researcher bias in an ethnographic report', *Research in Education*, **50**, 1–4.

Dugger, W. E. Jr. and Newberry, P. B. (1997) *Technology for all Americans Project*. Reston, VA: International Technology Education Association.

Ginner, T. (1995) 'Perspectives and concepts in the Swedish National Curriculum for Technology', in K. Langer, M. Metzing and D. Wahl *Technology Education, Innovation and Management*. Berlin: Springer.

Hammersley, M. (1992) 'Some reflections on ethnography and validity', *International Journal of Qualitative Studies in Education*, **5**(3), 195–203.

Kyriacou, C. (1992) Unpublished paper on research methodology. York University.

NCC (1993) *Technology Programmes of Study and Attainment Targets: Recommendations of the National Curriculum Council*. York: National Curriculum Council.

Scarth, J. and Hammersley, M. (1986) 'Some problems in assessing the closedness of classroom tasks', in M. Hammersley (ed.) *Case Studies in Classroom Research*. Milton Keynes: Open University Press.

Shield, G. (1992) 'Learning through a process model of technology education', *The Journal of Epsilon Pi Tau*, **18**(2), 43–52.

Silberstein, M. and Tamir, P. (1991) 'The expert case study model: an alternative approach to the development of teacher education modules', *Journal of Education for Teaching*, **17**(2), 165–79.

Smithers, A. and Robinson, P. (1992) *Technology in The National Curriculum*. London: The Engineering Council.

Tesch, R. (1990) *Qualitative Research Analysis Types and Software Tools*. London: Falmer.

Yamazaki, S. (1999) *A comparative study between UK, Canada and Japan on the Structure of Problem Solving with Creative Designing and Making in Technology Education*. International Conference on Integrated Thinking in Technology Education, Tai Tung, Taiwan.

Chapter 5

Resourcing Design and Technology
John Cave

Background

It seems surprising that so little has been written about physical resources in education generally and in design and technology in particular. Generic resources such as computer-based integrated learning systems contain echoes of the 1960's teaching machines built on behaviourist theory. We know about the theory, but what happened to the machines? How were they used? What were the outcomes? We can ask similar questions about the curious accumulated equipment of many, if not most, design and technology departments. The answers are not always obvious.

Judging from the evidence provided by textbooks, the development, influence and use of physical resources in design and technology and its precursor subjects present rich pickings for historical research. Considering the speed of changes in this area of the curriculum during the last 30 years, it is all the more remarkable that so little has been written about a changing resource base that has both supported and, arguably, influenced subject development and pedagogy. There is a parallel here with the surprisingly neglected area of educational textbooks. Only recently has a new organization, the Textbook Colloquium, taken a serious interest in this most ubiquitous of resources.

Design and technology, notwithstanding its status as a new subject, has a long and complex history whose ghost still dwells in its resources. We use hand tools, machine tools and other industrial equipment and processes to make things. This activity largely takes place in specialized environments – called workshops – and uses materials, many of which have been in use in schools since the nineteenth century.

Early craft subject practitioners were confident about basic resource needs for a relatively stable subject that in many respects changed very little between 1900 and the 1960s. On the subject of hand tools and materials O. Salomon, the writer of *The Teachers' Handbook of Slojd* (1894), would recognize (and probably still agree with) much of what was written by Glenister in his classic *The Technique of Handicraft Teaching* of 1953.

The subject that became Craft, Design and Technology (CDT) in the 1970s was in part seeded by initiatives such as Project Technology and the Design and Craft Education Project. One strand of these developments led to control technology courses whose publications were premised on the use of new electrical/electronic and other systems. Shortly afterwards, the Schools Council publications for Modular Courses in Technology linked learning to the use of very specific resources ranging from pneumatic systems to mechanical construction kits. The take-up of modular technology was rapid and widespread judging from rising examination numbers and sales of textbooks. During this period, and leading up to the National Curriculum, the specialist environment itself began to change, fuelled in part by government grants to support initiatives such as the Training and Vocational Educational Initiative. Workshops gave way to 'clean areas' (to use one prevalent term) offering purpose-built benching carrying low voltage supplies and compressed air for use with specialized resources. In a very short time, physical resources had assumed a new, dominating role in subject delivery.

Modular examination courses encapsulated and articulated a particular view of teaching and learning: 'theory' could be taught efficiently using specialized resource kits and ideas which thus learnt, could be transferred and applied to design and make tasks. Around this time one can pick out other minor resource-dependent trends in CDT, for example the use of polyester resin for fabrication and casting, lapidiary work and jewellery making; materials based on the use of metallurgical test equipment. But prescribed and tightly structured project work in wood or metal was often simply extended to new materials. Although now regarded as a generic material in design and technology, early work in plastics, notably acrylic and polystyrene, echoed the technique-orientation of earlier craft work.

The theory

Historically, we can identify a variety of teaching and learning theories used to explain the significance of working with tools and materials. Glenister (1953), for example, articulated a faculty psychology view of cognitive development in which logical thinking (as a mental faculty) could be developed and sharpened through craft practice. This is a view that preceded Glenister and was embodied in many post-Glenister textbooks. On this view, 'proper engagement' with tools and materials was valuable whatever the actual medium. Indeed, one can still detect resonances of Glenister in arguments supporting the 'educational value' of design and technology.

The current theoretical anchor for design and technology is probably the Assessment of Performance Unit (APU) Report (see Kimbell *et al.* (1990)) which set the agenda for ideas such as 'capability' (as the goal for design and technology education) and originated the now classic mind/hand interaction model of process. This model emphasizes the significance of mental imagery (within the mind's eye) and its development through continuous 'practical' engagement. It is an elegant and persuasive model, but one that naturally invites further unpicking and elaboration. Help in doing this comes from a slightly unexpected quarter: the history of technology. Many of the APU's discussions and conclusions are more subsequently echoed in Ferguson (1992) which shows, incidentally, that the mind's eye metaphor in the context of design can be traced back to the fourteenth century. A more recent publication[1], examining the process of invention in relation to the telephone and other seminal artefacts, discusses the emerging notion of 'mechanical representations' which are characterized as more than just visual imagery. These are cognitive constructs, sometimes having physical counterparts, which are stored as a kind of vocabulary. Collectively, such representations of mechanisms, materials or processes constitute a distinctive way of knowing and understanding which can be brought to bear in solving problems. Durbin (1991) discusses the phenomena of 'phantasma' or sensory representation. Such discussions clearly raise fundamental issues about the nature of knowledge and creativity in design and technology.

If fully understanding the left-hand side of the APU learning process model presents a challenge, it is equally true of the right-hand side where interaction takes place with 'things', i.e. 'handling tools and manipulating materials to confront the reality of design proposals' (Kimbell *et al.*

(1990)). Unpicking this side of the model also raises more questions than answers, not least how can we contrive resources that best facilitate learning and capability?

As the scope of design and technology has broadened into areas such as electronics and control, specialized resources have become increasingly important. Some of the kits used during the last 30 years or so were previously used in science teaching; others were developed specially for the new (emerging) subject. The design and use of such resources, considered in relation to the APU model, raises important questions. For example, it was implicit in publications,[2] and certainly assumed by teachers at the time, that certain ideas to do with mechanisms, control and structures could be learnt most efficiently and effectively through assembly kits. Such knowledge and understanding would then be transferable to solving problems. There is a strong suspicion that it works but very little hard evidence about why or how.

Interestingly, this suspicion becomes a firm assertion in Petroski (1999) who argues, as indeed do many engineers, that growing up playing with mechanical toys such as Meccano was both a basic formative influence and a necessary component of becoming a capable engineer. He laments the fact that young people are generally less likely to have hands-on experience and points out an apparent consequence that American universities (e.g. Stanford) are now having to develop 'remedial play' courses to give a hands-on feel for how things work through taking them apart and reassembling them. This clearly has a resonance in the National Curriculum requirement for disassembly, but it also has implications for exposure to any physical resource which might now be encountered only during a formally taught course.

Case-study

It is perhaps too early to make sense of changes engendered by the introduction of the National Curriculum. Certainly, design and technology specialists now seem to share broad beliefs that, for example, design and technology is about engendering 'capability'. But philosophical and practical differences remain, and these often appear in the way physical resources are perceived and deployed.

There are currently three major curriculum initiatives in design and technology: the Nuffield Design and Technology Project, the Royal College of Art Schools Technology Project, and the Technology Enhancement Programme (TEP). Nuffield and RCA have produced a huge range of innovative individual-use textbooks; TEP has published primarily photocopiable texts allied closely to new physical resources. TEP is noticeably different in having invested heavily in the development of physical resources and clearly believes they contribute significantly to 'subject enhancement and enrichment'. Because of this emphasis on resources, TEP has been chosen as a case-study for this chapter.

TEP was set up in 1992 with funding from the Gatsby Charitable Foundation to 'enhance and enrich' technology education in schools. It was originally managed by the Engineering Council, but is now part of the Gatsby Technical Education Project. Early in the programme Middlesex University was contracted to edit publications and create physical resources to further the TEP mission of curriculum enrichment. TEP's original broad mission statement has translated into more specific goals, for example, to facilitate quality making; to enable schools to incorporate advanced technology and manufacturing in practical activities; to promote mathematics and science within design and technology.

The TEP publications portfolio includes several general texts containing project ideas which can be variously interpreted by teachers as focused tasks (as defined by Nuffield) or springboards for capability tasks (where capability is characterized, for example, as 'the rounded and comprehensive capacity to locate a design opportunity, formulate ideas, realise an idea and systematically evaluate its effectiveness'.)[3] The TEP range also contains specific publications relating to particular technologies, equipment or materials. It is useful to give some examples:

Manufacturing (Cave, 1985a), one of the first TEP foundation (ages 14–16) texts, provides detailed instructions supported by specially designed kits, for injection moulding small products using a hot melt glue gun instead of a conventional injection moulding machine. This was intended to provide pupils with access to a process normally involving expensive equipment and difficult mould making procedures. This system has now been further developed and enables near-commercial quality manufacturing of parts from supplied moulds or those designed and made by pupils.

Structures (Cave, 1985b), also a foundation text, sets out a formula for creating structural components from tightly rolled paper tubes ('roll-tubes') and making these into space frames. The cost is very low and provides hands-on experience of designing and making functional geodesic structures as opposed to models.

TEP's interest in control systems has resulted in three programmable control products: the 'bit by bit' controller (a controller having the characteristics of a programmable logic controller), a smartcard programming system and the Chip Factory (a device for programming PIC microcontroller chips). All these systems can be battery operated and enable control systems to be built into project work.

TEP has also made available a wide range of other resources, notably new materials such as a low-temperature thermoplastic (Polymorph), thermochromic film (which changes colour at 27°C), and smart memory alloy wires.

The Millennium Award-winning TEP CNC machine is a relatively inexpensive machine tool for illustrating the function of larger commercial machines and enabling schools to manufacture precision components on a small scale. In its original version, it was supplied with a self-contained controller offering the ease of use of a Big Track toy, a programmable toy from the 1980s.

Overall, a wide-ranging portfolio of resources has been designed and assembled with the intention of giving pupils and students access to actual commercial materials and resources, and the further possibility of representing commercial manufacturing and control techniques.

Although TEP is measuring the impact of its programme through ongoing independent studies (e.g. National Foundation for Educational Research), it is clear that these case-study examples invite many interesting questions, any one of which might lead to a significant line of research enquiry. The roll-tube system enables pupils to construct impressive (and attractive) space frames; this is clear from published accounts of its use. But what are pupils actually learning through the use of this system and how far is learning, either 'intuitive' or more formalized, transferable to thinking about larger-scale structures, and understanding real structures in the environment? Similarly, how far does the use of TEP's injection moulding system assist understanding of a fundamental manufacturing concept and provide a transferable skill, both of which are implied in the relevant publication?

The examples of structures and manufacturing are physical processes with visible outcomes. TEP's control system resources are designed to enable pupils to get a toe-hold into relatively abstract ideas such as programmable logic control which underpin many modern production line systems. The bit by bit controller provides a very simplified model in which single bits of information are entered, stored and used literally a single bit at a time. The underlying assumption here is that since most programmable systems use digital information, exposing pupils to programming procedures involving indivisible digital bits provides a more logical conceptual base than beginning with one of the higher-level programming languages which pupils are commonly introduced to through PC-based control packages. There is overwhelming anecdotal evidence that this approach is effective, but underlying assumptions remain largely untested. Further important questions follow: how effective, for example, are simplified protocols used in TEP's other control systems in developing generic understanding and how transferable are they to other systems? The Chip Factory deliberately sets out to avoid any need for proficiency in assembly code (the language of PIC microcontrollers) and translates automatically from a form of Basic whose vocabulary mirrors everyday usage ('if y then x follows'). In what ways does this approach support those who subsequently want to exploit the full functionality of PICs?

The CNC machine, while incorporating the main broader features of a commercial milling machine, offers simplified icon-assisted programming with which pupils will already be familiar on toys and consumer products. Again, there is strong anecdotal evidence showing that pupils can access the machine rapidly and that the imposed discipline of graphically planning X Y pathways develops knowledge and skills that can be transferred to similar and, indeed, different contexts. How this actually happens remains to be examined through further systematic investigation.

TEP has consistently argued that the availability of resources has not caught up with practical needs in a subject whose up-to-dateness is measured by those very resources. It is also suggested that the subject risks decoupling from the interests and perceptions of pupils who are increasingly consumers of ever cheaper but more sophisticated products. Much of TEP's resource base therefore attempts to reflect contemporary trends in the use of materials, manufacturing methods and design trends. In fact, although the TEP resource development programme is warmly welcomed by teachers, it may well be outstripping the curriculum's capacity for adaptation and change. A good example is the introduction of the Chip Factory which suddenly empowers pupils from Key Stage 3 to effectively design and manufacture their own chips. The solution to a control problem that once called for considerable expertise can now be worked out and programmed into a chip by pupils at Key Stage 3. Where does this leave differentiation?

The future, we are often told, is smart. We might add that it is changing at an alarming rate and nowhere is this more obvious than in technology. Can design and technology as a school subject reflect or cope with these changes? One trend is to make increasing use of software-based virtual resources either through CD-ROMs or the Internet. Without doubt, this is a significant trend but there is strong evidence that if the overall goal of design and technology is the development of capability, 'virtuality' is not sufficient.

If design and technology teaching continues its love affair with physical resources, then these will present greater challenges both to the resource designer and to the teacher managing change in the classroom. In an unpublished briefing paper[4] on future trends, TEP has identified several areas where, potentially, schools 'are lagging further behind (external) developments both in terms of teachers' awareness of change and schools delivery of design and technology programmes'.[5] The paper is based on commercial briefing documents and identifies the following areas:

- materials
- electronic/control systems
- machines/mechanisms/mechatronics
- manufacturing
- information exchange.

Most teachers will recognize the increasingly difficult problem of satisfying pupils' aspirations in project work. This is hardly surprising when they are significant consumers of products which employ new technologies and, often, exotic materials. Increasingly, video cameras and other products use sonic wave motors; 'intelligence' is routinely embedded in consumer products, and product development itself can involve any one of four established rapid prototyping techniques.

Conclusion

Design and technology is a subject which, more than most, uses physical resources. These cannot simply be viewed as a passive means to an end. They are designed with certain expectations, based on beliefs about teaching and learning, and interact in complex ways with the learner. Physical resources certainly seem to suggest new lines of research enquiry. They have a history worth exploring and they call out for systematic investigation into their uses and effectiveness. Yet, while underpinning the teaching of the subject, they nevertheless remain one of the least understood elements of it.

Notes

1. Webster, R. and Perkins, D. (1992) *Inventive minds: Creativity in Technology*. Oxford: Oxford University Press.
2. See for example Cave, J. (ed.) (1993) *Design and Technology Omnibus*. London: Engineering Council.
3. Cave, J. (1995) Technology Education Briefing Paper. London: CTC Trust.
4. Cave, J. (1998) *The Millennium and Technology Futures*. London: Middlesex University.
5. *Ibid.*

References

Cave, J. (ed.) (1985a) *Manufacturing 14–16*. London: TEP.

Cave, J. (ed.) (1985b) *Structures 14–16*. London: TEP.

Durbin, P. (ed.) (1991) *Critical Perspectives in Nonacademic Science and Engineering*. London: Associated Universities Press.

Furguson, E. (1992) *Engineering and the Mind's Eye*. MA: MIT Press.

Glenister, S. (1953) *The Technique of Handicraft Teaching*. London: Harrap.

Penfold, J. (1988) *Craft, Design & Technology: Past Present and Future*. Stoke on Trent: Trentham Books.

Petroski, H. (1999) 'Work and Play', *American Scientist*, 87(3), 17–19.

Salomon, O. (1894) *The Teachers' Handbook of Slojd*. London: George Philip.

Chapter 6

Developing Textbooks

Ian Holdsworth

Introduction

As a design and technology community we have never been truly successful in explaining our subject matter to the lay person, so perhaps we should
start by looking at how we have tried to explain it to ourselves. This chapter
sets out to seek the significance of design and technology in contemporary
society through the medium of the textbooks aimed at servicing the subject.

Our history of craft education is our culture's history of transmitting
technological capability. It is a long and complex journey that began to be
formalized in 1880, but which had a lengthy history before this date in
the form of the apprenticeship and guild systems. However we will take
this date, the inception of the Elementary Schools Education Act, as a
starting point.

Although it seems obvious to think of woodwork and metalwork as the
initiating subjects in craft education, this does not turn out to be the case.
There was one practical subject already well-established in the day schools
which was readily absorbed into the elementary schools; this was
needlework. Blatchford states:

> Among the Board's instructions to Inspectors in 1883 was included
> this directive: 'It is of great importance that teachers of all grades
> should give evidence of their power of teaching needlework by
> demonstration and by the "simultaneous method"'. Thus an estab-
> lished form of craft teaching for girls (both domestic economy and
> needlework) was an accepted responsibility of the national education
> system from the very beginning.
>
> (Blatchford, 1961, p. 21)

Needlework and its associated subject of domestic economy provided a craft education for girls that the prevailing Victorian values and attitudes demanded. The subject was designed to produce competence as homemakers (and therefore potential wives) in young ladies who had little prospect of entering commerce or industry. As a subject needlework had a large, taught making content encompassing such areas as needlepoint, sewing, pattern cutting and dressmaking and so was heavily skill and process-based. It led to direct, if highly structured made outcomes, and it is to be noted that the teachers of it had to demonstrate their own competence in the subject by teaching their pupils 'by the simultaneous method', i.e. by the rote copying of a teacher-led demonstration. This led to the concept of teaching by 'models' through consecutive, sequential and interrelated exercises. We shall see that these two methodologies permeate the original approaches to the subject.

Manual instruction and Slojd

Whilst girls had a readily accessible subject to undertake that required little in the provision of resources for its delivery, boys were still deprived of practical activity. This was due to the fact that the resourcing of a suitable subject, namely woodwork, lacked financial support and a methodology to teach it. It was not until the latter part of the 1880s that we saw the development of woodwork lessons for boys and the start of the application of the term 'manual instruction' to describe this type of activity. However, from the start there was confusion in the minds of the subject originators as to the reasons for teaching practical activity – was it to be educational or vocational? Young contradicts himself in an opening paragraph:

> The true aim of Manual Instruction is not to make mechanics, any more than the teaching of drawing is to make all pupils artists, but to give to all boys that training of hand, and eye, and muscle which is universally useful, and that foundation of mechanical skill which to many boys may be the beginning of their future occupations. As a school subject Manual Instruction must be educational in its methods, simple in its language, graded into easy stages, intelligent in all it possesses and suggestive in its constructive usefulness.
>
> (Young, c. 1900, Introduction)

To Young the subject may not have been 'to make mechanics' but to lay a foundation of skills for 'future occupations'. It was a confusion of philosophy that was to permeate the early history of the literature, as it still does to the present day. Is it the nature of the subject that has always begged the question *Why are we teaching this?* However at the turn of the twentieth century social geography had a sharpening focus on the provision of education. St John and Turrell remark:

> Carpentry is probably the most popular form of Manual Instruction adopted by the County Councils in their Technical Education Schemes. There are two classes of pupils to provide for. The first includes youths just left school, who in many cases have already had a course of lessons on the subject, and apprentices. In this case the course should be considered from an educational point of view. The pupils should make drawings, both isometric and to scale of each piece of work, and the work should be done to the drawings, the exercises carefully graduated, and great accuracy demanded. In the second case, village classes are often attended by agricultural labourers and others, who could not possibly be expected to do the drawings, and the course of instruction should be looked upon as a means of making the men handy.
>
> (St John and Turrell, *c.* 1915, back cover)

St John and Turrell give us a view of the social class/vocation debate. Vocational training is seen as educative whilst the 'agricultural labourers and others' seem only to need to gain life skills. The inference being that as these students are deemed to be the non-intellectual, for the less able who 'could not possibly be expected to do the drawings' there was no need for them to learn 'from an educational point of view'.

A fundamental impact on a philosophy for English craft education was to come from abroad. By the end of the nineteenth century most European countries were attempting to establish some form of practical instruction within their embryonic school systems, usually with little success. France, Germany, Denmark, Norway and Ireland all suffered failed attempts. Only in Sweden, and only initially through private finance and enthusiasm, did the form of craft education known as Slojd make any significant impact.

The word *Slojd* can be loosely translated to mean 'hand education' and is derived from the Swedish practice of carving wood (and to a lesser extent wroughting iron) to make useful artifacts during the long months of the Scandinavian winter. The translation of the word should embody the tacit understanding that this is an important act of cultural transmission and that the educational aspect is not only to be found within the learning of craft skill, but also in the passing on of knowledge through the generations. The word also contains connotations of domestic or home-based industry. For various economic and social reasons the practice of Slojd was in decline at the end of the nineteenth century and attempts were made to revive it through a number of training schemes.

One such scheme was started in 1872 on a private estate at Naas near Gothenburg by August Abrahamson and his nephew Otto Salomon. This was a programme of teacher training to bring Slojd back into folk industry, but rapidly developed into a craft education training programme for professional teachers. In this way Abrahamson and Salomon laid down the first conceptual framework for educational craftwork. By 1882 they were training teachers from most European countries including England, and by 1896 approximately half the schools in Sweden were using their techniques.

Salomon's contribution was to propose a general *modus operandi* for craft education in two books, *The Teachers' Handbook of Slojd* and *The Theory of Educational Slojd*, which were translated and published in England in 1894. As Blatchford states:

> Salomon was pre-eminently the pioneer educationalist in practical work. By his methodical, even pedantic approach, he evolved a technique by which the natural abilities of children could be developed through manual work without directly teaching them a trade.
>
> (Blatchford, 1961, p. 28)

What Salomon proposed were not only some basic and fairly obvious general rules for teaching but also some specific rules for teaching craft as a subject. These he summarized as:

- The instruction should be intuitive in character, i.e. it should be given as far as possible through the senses, especially touch and sight;
- The instructor should be a teacher and not an artisan;
- The (made) models must be useful from the child's standpoint;
- The work should not involve fatiguing preparatory exercises;
- The work must afford variety;
- Children must be capable of doing the work themselves;
- The work must be real work, not a pretence at it;
- The object made should become the property of the child.

(Blatchford, 1961, p. 28)

Figure 6.1 *(Reprinted from Salomon, 1894, p. 191)*

Salomon proposed the implementation of these rules through lessons, the simultaneous method and models. Lessons enabled the teaching of skills, techniques and processes through a formalistic, incremental methodology gradually introducing more complex ranges of tools and making procedures. This learning was then applied to making models. From this Salomon abstracted the notions of 'work Slojd' (which was to do with the learning of craft skills) and 'educational Slojd' (the development of the personal qualities of the child through craftsmanship).

The translation of a Scandinavian-based cultural craft form into an English educational experience was not without its difficulties or its detractors. Chief amongst the problems was the use of the Slojd knife as the introductory tool for working wood. Although an important tool in the hand carved approach to much Swedish craftwork, it had little place in the more formal constructional approach to English woodwork. Sutton, drawing on *The Theory of Educational Slojd* by 'an Inspector of Schools' published in 1894 states;

The types of models produced by wood-Slojd are revealing:

1. Curvilinear – Scoop ladle etc., tested principally by eye and touch
2. Rectilinear – Pin tray, cloak suspender, bracket, picture frame, small table, etc., tested with compass and square

These two types of work bear the same relation to one another as Freehand to Geometrical drawing. As Freehand comes first, so in Slojd, Curvilinear models are made. The controversy between 'curvilinear' – derived largely from the use of the knife – and 'rectilinear' – produced by carpenters' tools – was to develop in this country, and Slojd lost the day.

(Sutton, 1967, p. 181)

Barter (1892) also criticises the use of the knife:

One of the most important tools used in the Slojd course, and certainly the most unique is the Slojd knife . . . (however) . . . it has been found in this country that all work that can be done with the knife can be more efficiently performed with a chisel . . . Another more technical objection is the great use made of glass paper . . . the pupil is apt to be careless in his initial work.

(Barter, 1892, Introduction)

Philip Magnus, a key figure in the history of craft teaching in England at the turn of the twentieth century and who sat on the Technical Instruction Commission of the time states:

Let the pupil try and try again till his strokes are clean and true. In Slojd the knife, which is so freely used gives short undecided cuts, and the work is too often finished with glass paper, a method which tends to destroy that self reliance which should be one of the chief moral results of manual training. The models in Slojd are not so well adapted to illustrate correct geometric principles, or to train the student in the interpretation of working drawings, as the construction of joints or models exemplifying such joints. For this reason the system of woodworking generally adopted in this country is superior to the Slojd teaching of Sweden.

(Magnus, 1910, p. 19)

Or as Sutton puts it, quoting from an HMSO report of 1895:

Not surprisingly the Science and Art Department's support was for the 'Nameless English System' rather than for Slojd. 'The first essential in any form of manual instruction is accuracy' stated one of its inspectors. The flat surfaces bounded by straight lines could be far more easily tested for 'accuracy', therefore the English system was superior to the Swedish.

(Sutton, 1967, p. 186)

But if the rural craft aspects of Slojd lost something in translation into a English system of woodworking rich in cabinet making and carpentry skills, Salomon's contribution to the development of craft education on a European scale cannot be overlooked. His vision, and the unique opportunities he created to transmit it, must award him a founding place within the history of craft education.

By the turn of the century manual training had enough identity as a body of taught knowledge to begin to be thought of as a school 'subject'. The difficulties in its full implementation were a lack of coherent philosophy, methodology and financial support. If money was to be found it was to come from, or at least through, other already existing subject areas. Young states:

> The Royal Commission on the Elementary Education Act's 1890 Instructions to Inspectors states: 'The difficulty which has hitherto prevented the recognition of Manual Training, as part of the ordinary course of the elementary school, has been removed . . . . Although no special grant is made by this department for such instruction you will watch with care the working of any experiment which is made in this direction and will report upon it.' Although no grant was made by the Education Department the early experiments in manual training were given financial support by the Science and Art Department.
>
> <div align="right">(Young, <i>c.</i> 1910, Introduction)</div>

Where else would finance come from if not from Science and Art? It says much about trying to place practical activity into a school curriculum, this hybrid subject, part technical, part creative. It must have been to the immense chagrin of many scientists and artists to be asked to fund it; to them it would have come from the wrong side of Plato's tracks. But there was one area of agreement as to standard good practice. The methodology for teaching was to be a sequential and consecutive series of graded exercises, known as 'methods' or 'grades'. Analysis of the content of some of these methods gives an insight not only into the activities undertaken, but also the pedagogical philosophy of the teaching of making for the next 70 years.

The aim was to enable students to build up a repertoire of skills, each new skill being based upon that previously learnt. This was really no more than an application of the ways of teaching apprentices perpetuated by the guild system. Accuracy in marking out materials was considered of the highest importance, and the ability to read a rule a necessity, therefore presuming a certain amount of numerical ability. To aid in this development of accuracy a paper template was often first made and tested. An example from a contemporary textbook is given in Figure 6.2.

The preliminary manufacture of a paper template ascertained whether the student could actually read the drawing, to size the product, understand what was to be made, and understand what the product outcome was meant to be. This was usually also aided by the teacher showing a pre-made example of the product, with the students then being led by a series of step-by-step demonstrations through its manu-facture. The aim was entirely to develop a craft competency in concept-ual understanding of a three-dimensional object from a two-dimensional drawing, accuracy of measurement and marking out, removal of waste material through the relevant processes and, at a more advanced stage, fabrication using appropriate methods.

Judd's *Learn by Doing – A Scheme of Simple Woodwork*, published in 1905, provides us with an insight into texts available for the establishment of woodwork as a subject and the contemporary teaching method to deliver it. The book is a progressive scheme of woodwork teaching based on 'Frobelian ideals' with all making activity centred around the use of models. The models may be considered as the project work undertaken

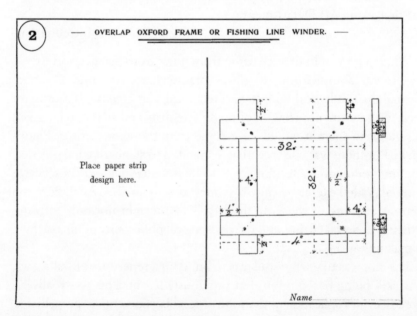

Figure 6.2 *(Reprinted from Judd, 1905, p. 77)*

by students as they are the making activities around which the suggested schemes of lessons are based. Judd includes models for first to fourth-year 'scholars', with alternative and advanced models for the brighter ones.

Judd suggests a graded programme starting with straight line 'wasting' exercises and ending with complex shaping and fabrication processes. The book shows examples of these models including string winder, fishing line winder, tee square, reversing spinning mill, a plant ladder, plant carrier, square frame, garden gate, step ladder, child's garden swing, garden seat, clothes airer, doll's bedstead, kitchen chair, doll's settle, wicket gate, cattle feeding manger, sack truck, wheel barrow and dog kennel followed by scale models of a field roller, harvest cart, merry-go-round, mechanical advertising machine, knife grinding machine, ore crushing, drop stamp machine, miner's hut or cabin, railway signals and steam motor car.

Handicraft

If manual instruction, followed by manual training, paved the way for school-based practical activity it was the emergence of the literature of handicraft in the 1920s that established a context for the educational activity 'making things'. Glass had his own definite ideas:

> Most children love to make things and should be encouraged to do so for many reasons. Craft lessons are of the greatest educational value, because they stimulate mental and motor activity simultaneously. It is generally admitted that when hand and brain are both employed much more is grasped and retained than when the brain alone is called upon to function. Furthermore, habits of industry are formed which are bound to be beneficial in the future. Children so trained are more likely to become useful and contented members of society in after-life than are those brought up with no craft instruction whatsoever.
>
> (Glass, 1928, p. 5)

But handicraft initially embraced a very wide range of making activities, exemplified by Farrington *et al.*, *Handicraft in the School* (undated, probably *c.* 1910), volume 3 of which contains junior, intermediate and senior courses on sand and clay modelling, bookbinding, leaded glass work and field geography. Not only does the early literature of the subject show that its scope was large but it originally contained elements of design activity. White and Watson state:

... in the light of modern educational thought craft teaching must be concentric and developed along a triple plan, comprising:

(a) a basic scheme;
(b) association with other subjects of the curriculum;
(c) association with the school as a whole and particularly with its cultural and aesthetic development.

(White and Watson, c. 1920, p. v)

They go on to suggest a first-year scheme of work associated with geography which would include:

Frames to hold sets of pictures which are interchangeable.
Frames to hold a sequence of seven maps each 30in by 22in.
Frieze made up of geographical pictures which have been framed in oak.
Model of a hill to illustrate contours together with a contoured plan and cross section.
Model to illustrate effect of lateral pressure of the earth.
Frames for two large maps of the world.

(White and Watson, c. 1920, p. 5)

But although handicraft remained a secondary school subject for some 50 years, it lost many of its original goals. Reliant on its concern with the transmission of craft skill it became woodwork, metalwork and needle-craft whilst spawning a plethora of textbooks that are now often derided. Over its lifetime some twenty handicraft textbooks a year were published for school use; this produced around 1,000 texts, of which Hooper and Shirley's *Handicraft in Wood and Metal* is a prime, early example both in layout and content. A sample is shown at Figure 6.3.

This genre of books, with some variations, continued well into the mid-1970s with individual authors applying their own aspirations to the subject. For example, although Hooper and Shirley produced a classic, model-based teaching manual they also considered that:

... at least one aspect of handicraft has been almost entirely neglected in the past, i.e. the artistic side; and, whilst not claiming any special merit for the design of the models dealt with, they have endeavoured to embody some artistic merit in the designs, and have tabooed the meaningless joints and collection of joints which have only a limited mechanical value. The general impression in the past has been that any attempt at 'freehand' curves or decoration in

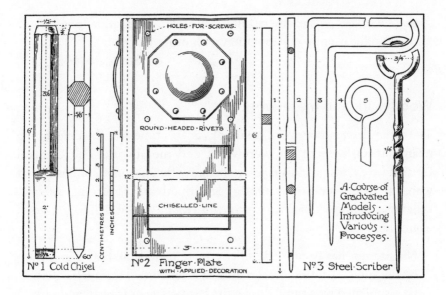

Figure 6.3 *(Reprinted from Hooper and Shirley, 1925, p. 67)*

models necessarily means neglect of the mechanical side, but this does not follow according to the authors' experience, and they would deplore the acceptance of this idea.

(Hooper and Shirley, 1925, Preface)

Throughout the history of handicraft, confusion grew as to why the subject was being taught. Although the textbooks might have dealt primarily with tools, materials, processes and technical information, the authors set their texts in a range of contexts – artistic, vocational, character forming and educational. Stoddard (1951) proposed the educational point of view:

Educational theory now recognises that the importance of handicraft lies not only in its practical nature, but also in its broad cultural influence. It provides a rare mental stimulus, offers scope for perseverance and patience, and gives an outlet to the creative urge, thus helping to prepare the student for the problems of life. The ideal, whether we work on the practical or the theoretical side of education, is to give scope to certain cravings, and to develop hidden talents which are inherent in us, talents insufficiently provided for even today in many school curricula. The aim of the handicraft teacher, therefore, should be not to try to make expert metalworkers or carpenters, but to lay a solid foundation for an all-round education in collaboration with other teachers.

(Stoddard, 1951, p. 7)

Woodwork and metalwork

The other driving feature of textbooks at this time was the developing examinations system for woodwork and metalwork. The General Certificate exams produced an opportunity for authors to publish what were in effect crammer textbooks aimed at resourcing specific syllabuses. King's *General Certificate Woodwork* of 1958 is a good example:

> No attempt has been made, of course, to include all that is known on the subject, but essential matter in a condensed form which can be assimilated by a pupil during the last two years (fourth and fifth forms) before the examination has been provided. Suitable exercises for tests or private study will be found at the end of each chapter.
>
> (King, 1958. p. 5)

A feature of 1950s and 1960s woodwork and metalwork textbooks was that their text be accompanied by line drawings. The annotated line drawings give them their particular character. Kettless's *Modern Woodwork* is a good example. A sample is shown at Figure 6.4.

Design and technology

The post-war years saw two developments; the rise of the use of 'new materials' and the development of a positive social attitude to design, both of which gradually became reflected in the subject literature, even if there was a considerable resistance to change, or as Rogers (1955) puts it:

> Design and schoolboys; we must not expect to get very far with this kind of thing in the secondary school.
>
> (Rogers, 1955, p. 4)

A surprising statement? Perhaps not for the time, remembering that the great majority of pupils engaged in making in resistant materials in secondary schools were boys and that the texts produced to support the activity were very male-centred and very directive in what was to be produced. Green, one of the authors of the Cassell's *Work Book* series states:

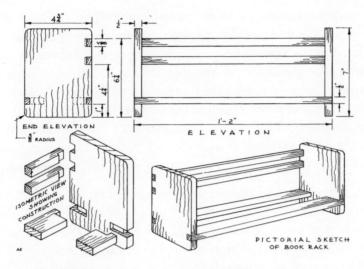

4 **Construction:**
(a) Well proportioned joints, adequate for the job.
(b) Decorative as well as functional possibilities of joints.
(c) Allowance for the natural movement of wood, and the combined use of solid and man made materials.

5 **Type of finish:**
(a) Suitability and characteristics of various finishes, e.g. in relation to use of article.
(b) French polish, wax polish, synthetic treatments, varnish and paint. See finishes pages 37 and 38.

Figure 6.4 *(Reprinted from Kettless, 1967, p. 64)*

SCULPTURE IN WOOD

Fig. 129 *(left)*. A duckling, in teak.
Height: 102 mm. (4 in.).
Made by a second-year pupil of below-average ability, aged 13 years.

Figure 6.5 *(Reprinted from Endean, 1969, p. 69)*

The modern emphasis on technical and handicraft education has made it possible for more than 80 per cent of the present generation of schoolboys to have a sound training in the working of metals in the normal course of their school lives . . . The models are simple. They were designed not for the few exceptional but for the large numbers of reasonably competent boys. There are no experiments. There is nothing which 'should' or 'might' work. Hundreds of boys have proved that they do work.

(Green, 1961, Introduction)

However design was a buzz word for post-war Britain and a number of attempts were made to integrate it into both art and craft teaching, often through carving wood. Almost as if the subject was looking for some tangible roots in its past the ideas of Slojd knife carving were reworked in a contemporary form, often using fish or animal motifs. Endean (1969) gives us a good example, with many connotations as shown in Figure 6.5.

Where books dealt with the use of new materials these generally revolved around the introduction of plastics, primarily acrylic sheet and casting resins, and also the use of manufactured boards. Plastics were seen as 'soft', easily worked and user friendly, whereas Parkinson (1967), a classic of the genre of mid-1960s project-based textbooks in its design and layout, realized the potential for the use of colour in plastics work:

Plastics, used separately or together with wood and metal, will provide greater scope for originality in design at all levels and will also introduce colour balance to the work.

(Parkinson, 1967, Preface)

It seems surprising that early books on the use of plastics in schools now seem so lacking in design content, concentrating on technical information rather than the application of the materials to project work. Clarke's (1970) *Plastics for Schools* discusses applied polymer science rather than practical outcomes that could be made by pupils. He approaches the subject from a need to know, technical information point of view, 'since polymers are becoming so important in our lives it is essential for people at school to know their capabilities and uses' (Foreword).

Birden and Hilsum (1973) took the same stance for, although their *Modern Materials for Workshop Projects* looks at a range of new materials for school use, including plastics, resins, glass reinforced plastics, man-made boards and aerated concrete, there is very little on what pupils might actually do with them. It is not until later into the 1970s, and with the emergence of the subject title design and technology, that we start to see a more integrated approach to design and materials technology. The Pergamon three-book series *Design and Technology: wood, metal and plastics* contained not only technical information, but also sections on design methodology. Millet (1977) makes the aim of the series explicit in his opening sentence, 'This book is intended to support the view that the study and practice of design are inseparable from the technology of materials' (Millett, 1977, p. 7).

Yarwood and Dunn (1979) went one stage further in producing a book that was primarily about design to help service the range of examinations that were available at the time. They perceived the need to break the mould of the standard textbook:

> The aim of the book is to describe in detail a systematic approach which can be applied to design and craft taught in schools. Craft techniques as such are not described in its pages.
>
> (Yarwood and Dunn, 1979, Preface)

This was a brave departure from the norm although the authors were careful not to ruffle too many feathers:

> The value of teaching traditional craft skills is fully recognised. When these craft skills are coupled to the intellectual challenge of solving design solutions, the educational value of craft teaching is greatly enhanced.
>
> (Yarwood and Dunn, 1979, Preface)

However, they not only had to place design in the subject context, they also had to find a way of articulating it:

> The design process strengthens the links which already exist between design, crafts and technical drawing. The technical drawing methods employed could be more properly referred to as technical graphics.
>
> (Yarwood and Dunn, 1979, Preface)

In fact Yarwood produced two books on graphical communication in the same year to underpin the concept of technical graphics as a move away from technical drawing.

One of the most influential set of textbooks to be published at this time were the Schools Council modular courses in technology which laid out in detail the technology areas of what was then CDT/D&T as a subject knowledge base. The set dealt with energy resources, electronics, mechanisms, structures, problem solving, materials technology, pneumatics and instrumentation with each area covered by a teacher's guide, workbook and filmstrip. Although technical in content, and containing assignments to do rather than projects to make, the books were some of the first to have a layout that used photographs as illustrations and the page mixture of text, line drawings and photographs created a model for later books.

CDT

The rise of CDT as a curriculum subject area in the 1980s saw many new authors grasping the opportunity to publish what their vision of the subject was, and how it should be resourced and delivered. A raft of new literature was produced very much following the layout model of text accompanied by line drawings and (sometimes colour) photographs. It is interesting to look at a number of textbooks from this period in an attempt to tease out what their authors were trying to express. Breckon and Prest (1983) give one example with their *Craft Design and Technology* which tries to set the scene for its content by asking:

> What is Craft, Design and Technology? Is it a new school subject? Is it three different subjects? Or is it one subject which involves a range of knowledge and skills?
>
> (Breckon and Prest, 1983, p. 4)

The authors continue with what is perhaps one of the few truisms that can be read from most of the literature of this time:

> Craft, Design and Technology is about designing and making things. It is not really new, although the title may be new in your school.
>
> (Breckon and Prest, 1983, p. 4)

Yarwood and Orme (1983) in their *Design and Technology* are more driven by a change process:

> One aim of this book is to show how a design process can be applied to the solution of projects in school technology. A second aim is to demonstrate that a school technology course can be fully developed from design and craft courses.
>
> (Yarwood and Orme, 1983, Preface)

Dunn's (1986) *Craft Design and Technology* develops the idea:

This book . . . is suitable for anybody who is being introduced to:

1   The design process (or problem solving)
2   Craft skills in wood, metal or plastics
3   The technologies of materials, structures, mechanisms, control with computers, electrics and electronics and energy.

(Dunn, 1986, Preface)

Whereas Kimbell's (1987) *Craft Design and Technology* aimed at resourcing the three CDT GCSE courses available at the time: CDT design and communication, CDT design and realization, and CDT technology. Without attempting to state what CDT is (apart from saying it 'encompasses an enormously broad field of study'), Kimbell abstracts from these three syllabuses 'common core' elements to base the book on:

This common core covers the basic principles of designing, making and communicating that are vital for studying any of the three CDT courses.

(Kimbell, 1987, p. 5)

The theme of a common core of activity supporting a particular field of study is taken up by Marden (1987) in his innovatively produced *Design and Realization* which places making in D&T within the parameters of problem solving using resistant materials:

This book aims to help design students to solve open ended problems . . . The book is divided into sections, the first of which deals with the design process, from the initial brief to the final evaluation. The remaining sections are arranged in the form of a manual, from which students can select materials, tools, processes, technologies and drawing systems, as and when they are needed.

(Marden, 1987, p. 3)

The design problem approach is echoed by Williamson and Sharpe in their *CDT in context*:

(this book) will encourage you to look carefully at situations and problems and advise you how to investigate them. Questions and drawings suggest how you can develop your ideas. There is guidance on the planning, making and testing of your solutions.

(Williamson and Sharpe, 1988, p. 3)

Cave (1986), *Technology in School – A Handbook of Practical Approaches and Ideas*, promoted the idea of a higher applied technology content:

> Essentially an ideas resource book, this text is designed specifically for Craft, Design and Technology teachers in schools who want to introduce a larger element of technology into their teaching at all levels . . . Technology in school is currently one of the fastest growing areas in the curriculum and appropriate resource material is constantly in demand.
>
> (Cave, 1986, back cover)

We see, therefore, that by the end of the 1980s CDT/D&T subject texts revolve around the content of designing (problem solving), making (tools, materials and processes) and the application of technologies (mechanisms, electronics, structures, computer control, etc.) These three areas were well developed in the three-book *Collins CDT* series which dealt with design and communication, design and realization and technology. The introduction to *Design and Realisation* (Chapman and Peace, 1988) seems to sum up the scope of the series:

> This book is based on the principle that CDT is an activity focussed area of the curriculum concerned with designing and making artefacts and/or systems to meet a specific purpose . . . . An important feature of the book is to place CDT in the context of the world in which we live.
>
> (Chapman and Peace, 1988, p. iv)

Placing D&T in a 'real world' context is a theme taken up by Caborn, Mould and Cave (1989) in their *Design and Technology*:

> The term 'design and technology' is used to describe a wide range of activities . . . There are therefore many answers to the question, 'What is design and technology?', and it is very easy to become confused. All the activities grouped under the title design and technology do, however, share a number of common features: identifying a problem, thinking about it and realising a solution. Improving an electronic circuit, designing a piece of furniture and creating a new range of clothing all have problem solving in common.
>
> (Caborn *et al.*, 1989, p. 1)

Conclusion

The introduction of the National Curriculum for design and technology in the 1990s introduced the concept of four fields of knowledge for D&T plus a common core, giving authors new and specific targets to write for. Leading the literature to resource D&T National Curriculum requirements have been the three national research projects into the area – the Royal College of Art Schools Technology Project, The Nuffield Design and Technology Project and the Technology Enhancement Programme. Each has produced text-based resource materials, although in the case of the RCA and Nuffield they are much wider in scope than textbooks, with only TEP following a tradition of technical information conveyed through text and line drawings.

So what of the future – are textbooks dead? I think not. As design and technology educators we have a rich bibliographical base to draw from, a wealth of literature that has developed along with the subject. That this literature does not follow the common methodologies or content, or that we may not all be 'singing from the same hymn sheet' may be confusing to the outsider, but does add to D&T's richness. Our subject has mirrored technological developments and society's appreciation of its products. The textbooks reflect this; they are accessible, informative and easy to use – attributes that may, hopefully, be applied to CDs and other forms of electronic media in the future.

References

Barter, S. (1892) *Woodwork (The English Slojd)*. London: Whittaker.

Birden, F. G. and Hilsum, J. (1973) *Modern Materials for Workshop Projects*. London: Hutchinson.

Blatchford, G. (1961) *A History of Handicraft Teaching*. London: Chatto and Windus.

Breckon, A. and Prest, D. (1983) *Craft Design and Technology*. London: Hutchinson.

Caborn, C., Mould, I. and Cave, J. (1989) *Design and Technology*. Walton on Thames: Nelson.

Cave, J. (1986) *Technology in School – A Handbook of Practical Approaches and Ideas*. London: Routledge and Kegan Paul.

Chapman, C. and Peace, M. (Breckon, A. ed.) (1988) *Design and Realisation*. London: Collins.

Clarke, P. J. (1970) *Plastics for Schools*. London: Mills and Boon.

Dunn, S. (1986) *Craft Design and Technology*. London: Bell and Hayman.

Endean, W. H. (1969) *Woodwork ideas for Teachers and Students*. Edinburgh: Technical Press.

Farrington, F. W. (*c.* 1910) *Handicraft in the School*. London: Gresham.

Glass, F. W. (1928) *Metal Craft*. London: University of London Press.

Green, I. W. (1961) *Cassell's Work Books No. 5 – Steam Powered Boats*. London: Cassell.

Hooper, J. and Shirley, A. (1925) *Handicraft in Wood and Metal*. London: Batsford.

Judd, H. J. (1905) *Learn by Doing – A Scheme of Simple Woodwork*. Manchester: Clarkson and Griffiths.

Kettless, A. W. P. (1967) *Modern Woodwork*. London: Macmillan.

Kimbell, R. (1987) *Craft Design and Technology*. London: Hutchinson.

King, H. E. (1958) *General Certificate Woodwork*. London: Harrap.

Magnus, Sir P. (1910) *Educational Aims and Efforts 1880–1910*. London: Longman.

Marden, A. (1987) *Design and Realization*. Oxford: Oxford University Press.

Millet, R. (1977) *Design and Technology Plastics*. Exeter: Wheaton.

Parkinson, K. (1967) *Projects and Design in Metalwork and Other Media*. Exeter: Wheaton.

Rogers, N. R. (1955) *Woodwork and Metalwork for Schools*. London: Pitman.

Salomon, O. (1894a) *The Teachers' Handbook of Slojd*. London: George Philip.

Salomon, O. (1894b) *The Theory of Educational Slojd*. London: Dent.

St John, G. and Turrell, W. M. (*c.* 1915) *The County Council Course of Manual Instruction*. London: Simpkin Marshall.

Stoddard, H. W. (1951) *Constructive Art Metalwork*. London: Dent.

Sutton, G. (1967) *Artisan or Artist*. Oxford: Pergamon Press.

White, W. B. and Watson, T. (*c.* 1920) *Handicraft in the Senior School*. London: University of London Press.

Williamson, D. and Sharpe, T. (1988) *CDT in Context*. London: Longman.

Yarwood, A. (1979) *Graphical Communication Book 1* and *Book 2*. Walton on Thames: Nelson.

Yarwood, A. and Dunn, S. (1979) *Design and Craft*. London: Hodder and Stoughton.

Yarwood, A. and Orme, A. H. (1983) *Design and Technology*. London: Hodder and Stoughton.

Young, C. S. (*c.* 1900) *Manual Training for the Standards*. London: Bean.

Chapter 7

Perspectives on Departmental Organization and Children's Learning through the Nuffield Design and Technology Project

David Barlex

The influence of the Nuffield Design and Technology Project on the revision of the Statutory Order

The Nuffield Design and Technology Project is a major curriculum development project that has published materials for both teachers and pupils. The project was initiated in 1990 as schools were required to teach design and technology for the first time. It soon became clear that many teachers were finding it extremely difficult to meet the new requirements. This was echoed by the finding of Her Majesty's Inspectors of Schools (HMI). The annual reports for design and technology in 1990 and 1991 (DES/Welsh Office, 1991, 1992) make sorry reading, showing a decline in pupils' ability to design and make since the introduction of the National Curriculum, particularly in the 11–14 age range. The project director realized that a three-pronged approach was necessary to solve the problem:

- the Statutory Order needed radical revision if it was to be understood by teachers;
- the subject needed a clear pedagogy that teachers could use to teach effectively;
- teachers needed curriculum materials that utilized the effective pedagogy and provided the detail lacking from the Order in a way that gave them ownership of the curriculum they had to teach.

The project worked closely with government departments and officials, particularly the review team led by HMI Vic Green that was set up to provide the first revision of the Order in 1992 (National Curriculum Council) and then with Mick Walker and Niel McLean, design and technology subject officers with the Schools Curriculum and Assessment Authority. The project convinced those responsible for revising the design and technology curriculum that much of the pedagogy developed by the project could be adopted nationally. This pedagogy consisted of three types of activities:

- *Resource Tasks* – short practical activities to make pupils think and help them learn the knowledge and skill they need to design and make really well.
- *Case-Studies* – true stories about design and technology in the world outside school. Pupils learn the way firms and businesses design and manufacture goods and how goods are marketed and sold. They also learn about the impact that products have on the people who use them and the places where they are made.
- *Capability Tasks* – designing and making a product that works. These build on the learning experience of Resource Tasks and Case-Studies.

The project argued that all three types of learning activity are necessary. Resource tasks and case-studies put pupils on the road to success, demonstrated through the challenge set up by the capability tasks. A diet of resource tasks and case-studies alone would not require the pupils to be capable. A diet of capability tasks alone would not give pupils the resources with which to be capable. By teaching through a mixed diet of these activities, teachers can ensure that their pupils are able to respond positively and effectively to the challenges of designing and making. The project saw the basis of curriculum planning for design and technology as identifying a sequence of capability tasks for pupils aged 11 to 14 years which provided breadth, balance, coherence and progression.

The pedagogy proposed by the Nuffield Project clearly influenced the teaching methods recommended in the revised Order of 1995 (SCAA, 1995). Resource tasks can be used as focused practical tasks (FPTs) and for investigation, disassembly and evaluation activities (IDEAs). Capability tasks can be used for designing and making assignments (DMAs). Case-study work was not formally adopted in the 1995 Revised Order for Design and Technology and this was a disappointment to the project. The project argued that to restrict teaching to a consideration of existing products and the designing and making of products was to limit pupils' experience of design and technology. Case-study work enabled pupils to consider large technologies such as communication systems, intermediate technology, technologies of the past, and the development and impact of powerful technologies (e.g. printing). Although elements of the programme of study might usefully be taught through case-study work, this was not a recommendation. However, the project took some satisfaction from the inclusion of case-study tasks as a recommended teaching method in the technology curriculum for Scotland (The Scottish Office Education Department, 1993).

Capability – the purpose of the teaching

The revised National Curriculum in England and Wales paints an impressive picture of the attributes developed through a good design and technology education. One sentence in particular captures the essence of capability in design and technology:

> Pupils learn to become autonomous, creative, problem solvers both as individuals and in working with others.
>
> (QCA/DfEE, 1999)

This chapter will now consider how departmental organization and children's learning can be focused to achieve these features. It is divided into two parts. The first considers the role of the individual teacher in providing effective teaching. The second part considers the issues involved in developing a team approach to teaching across a department.

The role of the individual teacher

The ground rules

There are four conditions that a teacher needs to meet if their teaching of design and technology is to be successful:

1. The teacher should have the expectation that pupils will be capable. This means that it will be perfectly acceptable for

pupils to make decisions and take action based on those decisions. In some cases the actions will require teacher approval but in many cases they will be autonomous.

2.   The teacher needs to facilitate pupil capability by organizing and maintaining an appropriate environment. This means that pupils will have open access to materials, components, tools and equipment. In most cases they will be able to collect what they need, as they need it, use it and return it. In some cases particularly scarce resources may need to be booked in advance. But it is essential that decisions, once taken, can be acted upon if pupils are not to become dispirited and demotivated.

3.   The teacher will need to provide the resources for capability by teaching the technical knowledge and understanding, aesthetics, design strategies, making and manufacturing skills and values needed for successful designing and making.

4.   The teacher should maintain the motivation for capability through insight into pupils' motivations, ensuring that activities are relevant, urgent, important and attractive.

Ensuring effective use of the teaching methods

The *Nuffield Design and Technology Teacher's Handbook* (Barlex *et al.*, 2000) gives clear guidance on how to make effective use of each of the teaching methods developed by the project and is useful for teaching design and technology as required by the revised National Curriculum.

For resource tasks it recommends that the teacher explains to pupils why they should do them. The explanation is simple. A teacher can say this to the class:

> Through Resource Tasks you will learn all sorts of stuff that will help you when you come to design and make things. The idea is that I help you a lot when you're doing resource tasks so that when you get to do a capability task – that's designing and making something – you won't need me to help you anything like as much, if at all. This is the game plan: we'll spend five weeks maximum doing resource tasks, maybe less if you can do them well *and* quickly; then we'll spend seven weeks on the capability task when you can show me just how good you are and how you can use what you've learned. Look at the chart over here and you'll see that I've put the

dates of the lessons that we're doing the different resource tasks leading up to the capability task and then all the lessons for the capability task. We can keep check on our progress.

The handbook gives clear guidance on practical organization of resource task work:

- each pupil should have a copy of the instruction sheets;
- each pupil should have a copy of any sheets that have to be filled in or cut up during the task; make sure that some spares are available for rectifying mistakes;
- allow sufficient time and if necessary deviate from the recommended time;
- ensure that the required materials, tools, and equipment are readily available;
- use a circus approach within your classroom to avoid equipment bottlenecks;
- if necessary go through the task with the class beforehand so that all pupils have clear targets for doing and writing;
- once the pupils are tackling the task, support them by asking questions, giving assistance, looking at what they write and draw and providing encouragement.

For case-studies it explains the possible purposes as follows:

- as a starting point for a product analysis exercise and as background to a product evaluation Resource Task;
- to provide background information for a Capability Task;
- to help provide technical understanding;
- to show the way designers and manufacturers do things;
- to provide the opportunity to evaluate the effects of design and technology in action.

The handbook also describes how the case studies are structured to make the reading an active exercise by using three types of activity:

- Pause for thought: this helps pupils to think about what they have just read so that the following text will be easier to understand. There is no need for pupils to write a response.

- Question: this asks the pupil to stop reading and to tackle the questions. The range of possible answers is wide. The pupil may need to write down an answer, make a drawing or a model, discuss the study with other pupils or make a short presentation to the class.
- Research: this asks the pupils to find out more and to write about what they have found out. It may involve using other information sources or talking to an expert. It may take quite a lot of time so pupils probably need to do it as homework.

Photocopy case-studies can be made even more active by employing Direct Action Related to Text (DART) techniques. As the case-studies are copies, pupils can carry out the following useful activities:

- underlining important words;
- making notes in the margin;
- cutting out pictures, sticking them onto a large piece of paper and adding notes; and
- colour coding words or phrases to do with a particular issue.

In addition, pupils can take them home, which is not always possible with textbooks which might be in short supply.

For Capability Tasks the handbook recommends that the teacher uses ten questions to plan the teaching.

1. *How should I introduce the task?* Eight different ways of introducing the task are discussed, each designed to provide an intriguing and motivating beginning.
2. *Do I link the task with other subjects?* To ensure that the majority of pupils make good use of other subjects, it is recommended that the teacher chooses a definite subject that lends itself to links with the capability task and then to teach that task with this in mind.
3. *How open do I make the brief?* The teacher is given guidance as to the openness of the brief. The more open the brief the wider the range of products pupils in a class will want to design and make. It is important that the brief is not so open that the teacher cannot support different pupils' attempts at designing

and making. It is important that the brief is not so closed that all pupils end up designing and making very similar products. It is essential that the individual signature of the pupil can show through the work.

4. *How do I ensure good design ideas?* It is suggested that the teacher deliberately limits the number of ideas pupils are asked to produce, noting the importance of feedback on these ideas. It suggests that each pupil is asked to produce one idea on a large 'post-it' note, the notes can be displayed and each pupil can get feedback from the rest of the group. In this way all pupils receive feedback and can adapt their ideas accordingly.

5. *How complex should the specification be?* It is suggested that able pupils should be working to more ambitious specifications than less-able pupils and that the teacher negotiates the detail with individual pupils as a good way to achieve differentiation.

6. *How will pupils model solutions?* Here the teacher is asked to decide on the diversity of experience that is appropriate and manageable. How many different sorts of modelling will be taking place in the class to produce prototype products (e.g. sketching, 3D mock-ups, working models, computer images)?

7. *How do I ensure they stay on track?* Here the teacher is asked to consider how the design ideas are scrutinized and it is suggested that this process can be made more dynamic by pupils working in pairs, taking on alternate roles of client and designer. The client has the specification and the designer the prototype product in whatever form this has been developed. The client has to question the designer about the prototype. The teacher can provide questions or expect the pupils to make them up. It is important that this feedback informs the final design.

8. *What sort of written feedback do I give?* Here the teacher is advised to give three-point feedback to each pupil based on their 'flat work' and any prototypes they have produced:
   — a comment about the design, either overall or a point of detail;
   — a comment about the production, where particular care is necessary for example;
   — a comment to motivate, personal to the pupil.

9. *How do I ensure quality making?* Here the teacher is advised to consider the range of tools, equipment, materials and

components they can use and the amount of help the teacher can give. The teacher may need to demonstrate or set up specialist making stations. It might be important to encourage pupils to help each other.

10. *How will I organize final evaluation?*   Several different strategies for final evaluation are considered:
    - comparison of performance against specification;
    - user response;
    - performance in the light of wider issues (winners and losers or appropriateness).

It is noted that these can be carried out by individuals, in pairs or small groups and sometimes through general class discussion and that pupils should be taught these methods of evaluating and given the opportunity to use them in a variety of ways.

Developing a team approach

Acknowledging the diversity

It is essential that the teachers working within a design and technology department operate as a team. This is not always easy as different members of the team are likely to have strong and differing opinions as to what is and is not important in the teaching of design and technology. It would be odd if this were otherwise particularly when we consider the different traditions and career paths that have contributed to the make up of the current teaching force. The teachers shown in Figure 7.1 are expressing their views as to the most important feature of design and technology education with special reference to designing and making. No-one would argue with the significance of the features: aesthetics, communicating skills, design procedures, making skills, or technical understanding, and values. Some would argue that to consider design and technology solely in terms of pupils' designing and making is limiting. What is essential is that none of these features dominates the way a department teaches pupils through designing and making. An over-emphasis or under-emphasis can lead to a skewed experience and a lack of breadth and balance. Clearly the head of department has a key role in enabling teachers to articulate their strongly held views in the context of a team approach so that each teacher feels valued and is able to

Figure 7.1 *Strongly held views that help shape the design and technology curriculum*

contribute appropriately to developing a broad and balanced approach to design and technology.

Cooperation between teachers through a subject construct model

A model for the personal construction of the subject for teachers has been developed by work at Brunel University and the Open University (Banks and Barlex, 1999). This model is summarized by the diagram in Figure 7.2. It involves three elements – subject knowledge, pedagogic knowledge and school knowledge. So the model indicates that teachers should 'know their stuff' (subject knowledge); 'know how to teach their stuff' (pedagogic knowledge) and 'know how to teach their stuff in their school' (school knowledge).

This is a useful way of looking at a subject, whatever it happens to be, but particularly so for design and technology because it is relatively new and there is still considerable uncertainty about its exact nature for many teachers. This is not surprising. In addition to being new, design and technology has to reflect to some extent a rapidly changing world in which technology and changes in technology are playing a major part. This model gives teachers and heads of department a valuable tool for looking at their practices, both as individuals and as teams. By reflecting on each of the features a team can build an effective agenda for both change and the support of in-service training. In looking at subject knowledge teachers can identify the strengths and weaknesses in the department and the professional development required for different individuals to address these issues. If in-service training is seen in the context of whole-team development, as well as individual development, the inevitable disruption caused by absence through course attendance will be minimized. For instance, if a member of staff attends a course on computer aided design and computer assisted manufacture (CADCAM) when this has been identified as an area of weakness in the D&T curriculum, the expertise acquired by that member of staff will be seen as valuable to the whole department. He or she will have the responsibility of teaching others about what has been learned on the course and helping all members of the department build CADCAM into the curriculum.

In looking at pedagogic knowledge teachers identify the range of methods used by colleagues across the department and through discussion and observation widen individual repertoires. For example, a member of staff may be particularly adept at whole-class teaching whilst

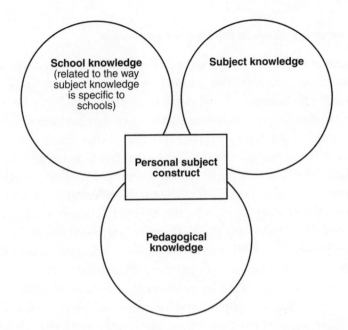

Figure 7.2 *A simple model for the personal construction of the subject for teachers*

another colleague may be expert at dealing with small groups. If a teacher is finding either of these activities difficult then observing the colleague with that expertise is an important and effective way of developing these teaching skills.

In looking at school knowledge teachers may ask the questions *Why do we do things this way?* and *What about doing them that way?* This is particularly important where the issue concerned is one that relates to whole-school policy, as in the case of assessment for example. The school policy may be that all work is graded with an effort and an attainment grade. It is important that the teachers within the D&T department have a clear and shared understanding of the meaning of the different grades for each of these features and also of what is required of pupils to make progress from one grade to the next. It may be that a department through discussion feels that grading is inappropriate and that comments describing clear targets for improvement are a better way of assessing pupils' work. In this case it is important for the department to discuss this difference of professional opinion with members of the senior management team before altering the department's assessment policy.

How a department might think about assessment

It is important that the assessment scheme used by the department is in line with school policy and that it meets the needs of teaching and learning in design and technology. Clearly it will be important for both the teacher and the pupil to keep records showing the work that has been completed. This may be in the form of a checklist that shows the resource tasks completed, the case-studies read and the capability tasks tackled. Each can be ticked off. This is simple record keeping and can probably be computerized. It is important that the pupil understands how to make best use of this work in developing their attainment in design and technology. The advice from the Nuffield Project, based on good research evidence (Williams, 1998) is to assess pupils' work rather than marking it. This can form the basis of a departmental meeting.

Conversations supported by short written comments added to the work whilst talking to a pupil during resource task and case-study work will be more useful than comments written on the work after collection. Similarly, conversations supported by short written comments during capability tasks will be useful. Key written comments after the second review of a capability task will also be particularly useful.

The question thus becomes one of looking at practice and establishing how to organize lessons so that such activity takes priority. Teachers working in pairs carrying out mutual observation is one method for a department to scrutinize practice in a way that is non-threatening yet highly focused.

Identifying clear targets for improvement by helping pupils to use the self-assessment sheets will be helpful. Here the issue becomes one of teachers themselves being clear about what it means to improve, and of helping pupils understand this for themselves. This is particularly important when pupils move from teacher to teacher across different media areas. Most targets for improvement should be generic and travel with the pupil to the next teacher. This can only be achieved if teachers have discussed the issues, come to an agreement on what improvement entails, and identified ways in which individual pupil targets can be communicated effectively and efficiently.

These forms of assessment enable teachers to write portfolio summaries of pupils' achievements that give ample evidence to report what each pupil has done, how well they have done it and what they should do to improve.

It has been noted that 'teachers are caught up in a culture of diligence. The recording of assessment data has become a burden because teachers do it so well' (Adams, 1999, p. 113). Those responsible for the Nuffield approach to assessment believe it will reduce the burden and allow diligence to be so focused that it is not wearisome.

Conclusion

This chapter began by considering briefly the influence of the Nuffield Design and Technology Project on the revision of the National Curriculum Order and the defining of capability by that Order. Next it considered how the individual teacher might maintain an appropriate learning environment and use the Nuffield Design and Technology interpretation of recommended pedagogies to develop pupils' capability. Finally it discussed the way teachers might construct their knowledge of the subject they teach and how this may be used to facilitate a cooperative approach to effective teaching across a department.

References

Banks, F. and Barlex, D. (1999) 'No one forgets a good teacher', *Journal of Design and Technology Education*, **4**(3), 223.

Barlex, D. *et al.* (2000) *Nuffield Design and Technology Teacher's Handbook*. London: Longman.

Black, P. and William, D. (1998) *Inside the Black Box: Raising Standards through Classroom Assessment*. London: Kings College School of Education.

Carol Adams, Chief Officer, General Teachers' Council, quoted in Robinson (1999) *All Our Futures: Creativity, Culture and Education*. London, National Advisory Committee on Creative and Cultural Education.

DES/Welsh Office (1991, 1992) *Design and Technology in Secondary Schools*. HMI Reports (1991 and 1992). London: HMSO.

National Curriculum Council (1992) *Technology for ages 5 to 16*. DES/Welsh Office.

QCA/DfEE (1999) *The Review of the National Curriculum in England – The Consultation Materials*. London: Qualifications and Curriculum Authority.

SCAA (1995) *Design and Technology in the National Curriculum*. London: School Curriculum and Assessment Authority.

Scottish Office Education Department (1993) *Curriculum and Assessment in Scotland: National Guidelines, Environmental Studies 5–14*. Edinburgh: The Scottish Office Education Department.

Chapter 8

The Introduction of Criterion-Referenced Assessment to Design and Technology

Richard Tufnell

Introduction

The National Curriculum introduced in 1988 required that pupils' achievements should be measured and reported at regular intervals. This chapter is drawn from research which investigated and developed statutory assessments in design and technology at the end of Key Stage 3, normally after nine years of schooling. Design and technology, as defined by the National Curriculum, represented a significant change for the majority of schools' philosophy, subject content and organization, and particularly in the context of this chapter, assessment. Consequently, expertise and resources needed to be focused on the development of assessment procedures especially given that the National Curriculum is based on criterion referencing which only recognizes and records pupils' positive achievements.

In order to produce reliable and valid assessments, successive trialling and piloting took place over a four-year period. This research resulted in a number of innovative approaches to criterion-referenced assessment, sufficiently robust for statutory assessment. As a consequence, the repertoire of assessment in design and technology was significantly extended. The research was required to serve both political and educational objectives; consequently, devising assessment procedures to meet their respective demands required compromise. Strategies have been identified which have been of value in the assessment of this subject both in the context of the National Curriculum and also in vocational and occupational contexts.

The case-study for criterion-referenced assessment

The National Curriculum was the first formal assessment procedure to adopt a truly criterion-referenced approach to the assessment of design and technology and led the way in making the approach available for a wide range of vocational and occupational assessment procedures in schools and further education institutions.

The commitment to this approach came 25 years after Glaser (1963) had published his seminal paper on this approach to assessment. He defined criterion-referenced assessment as:

> Measures which assess student achievement in terms of a criterion standard thus provide information as to the degree of competence attained by a particular student which is independent of reference to the performance of others.
>
> (Glaser, 1963, p. 32)

In this approach, the measurement of learning is described by what learners can do, rather than how well they have performed in relation to others or as a description of the learning input. A bank of criterion-referenced statements arranged in levels according to difficulty is, in effect, equivalent to a desired set of learning outcomes. A teacher faced with the task of planning the delivery of a Key Stage might use selected statements of attainment as the objectives of components of his or her teaching. In addition, statements of attainment are better motivators than syllabuses as they set pupils clear targets; the pupils know what is being asked of them. Uniting teaching objectives and assessment allows assessment to support learning and provide greater clarity of curriculum definition.

Traditionally, assessment in design and technology has been largely on the basis of outcome alone. Every pupil would be set the same task and marks would be awarded on the basis of the solution produced. More often than not, this was the result of the teacher norm-referencing within the group. Teacher judgements were probably highly reliable in the relationship of one individual to another, but this approach was not viable and could not be sustained given the introduction of level-related statements of attainment. The adoption of a multi-level scale of achievement was an ambitious enterprise. Such scales established sets of explicit criteria defining progress for pupils from 5 to 16. They implied that a pupil would, in each attainment target, sequentially progress from one level to the next, as they were systematically taught the demands of each level. However, learning is not that straightforward and teaching is rarely that systematic! The scales also presupposed that the content of the attainment targets was hierarchical. As design and technology capability defined a process, the assumption was that each level described a more complex and sophisticated activity which required the employment of more demanding skills and greater depth of subject knowledge. The complexity of defining these criteria so that they were applicable to pupils over their eleven years of schooling and could be interpreted consistently by teachers was underestimated.

Determining the nature of the assessment

Capability is the focus of design and technology assessment because, in a succinct and elegant fashion, it exemplifies the objectives of the subject. Since this is the accepted objective of the subject, it can be powerfully argued that any assessment procedure should concord with this approach. National Curriculum assessment was driven by the developments in mathematics and science; subjects constrained to testing only the knowledge component. Such an approach was, from the outset, at odds with the notion of design and technology capability. Assessment models more sensitive to 'purposeful activity' were being developed elsewhere during this period, particularly in relation to vocational qualifications. These models were extremely relevant to design and technology as it was one of the key subjects which might provide a vehicle for the introduction of vocational qualifications into the secondary sector. From the mid-1980s a new national system for the assessment of occupational competence was devised and introduced. National Vocational Qualifications (NVQs) are concerned with what an individual can do in the workplace. Competence is defined in specific terms:

> It is a description of an action, behaviour or outcome which the person should be able to demonstrate and it must be assessable.
>
> (NCVQ, 1991, p. 17)

This mode of assessment involves the collection and evaluation of evidence against performance criteria. An individual is required to demonstrate that his or her performance meets the prespecified standard. The notion of 'performance' is crucial to competence. It is not discussing or describing how something might be done, or the merits of doing it one way rather than another, but actually doing it. GNVQs (General National Vocational Qualifications) aimed to bridge the academic/vocational divide. These qualifications do not confirm occupational or professional competence. They are based, like the National Curriculum, on statements of attainment rather than statements of competence. NVQ assessment tasks must be undertaken in the workplace but this is not the case for GNVQs. In both, the assessment of learning outcomes must be appropriate and reflect the purpose of the course or programme of study.

This approach provided support for the notion that assessment should be in accordance with the character of the subject. In the case of design and technology this meant capability. Performance is as crucial to competence as it is to capability. The term 'authentic assessment' has been used by, amongst others, Goldstein (1994) to describe an interactive model of assessment which sees it as part of the learning procedure. Gipps (1994) confirmed that assessment tasks should be 'good examples of performance assessment. Performance assessments demand that the assessment tasks themselves are real examples of the skill or learning goals, rather than proxies' (p. 12). Resnick and Resnick (1992) observed, 'We cannot teach a skill component in one setting and expect it to be applied automatically in a context very different from the context from which it is practised or used' (p. 43).

What does 'authentic assessment' mean in the context of design and technology capability? Simply that all assessment tasks need to be purposeful activities undertaken in response to perceived needs or opportunities, within a context of specific constraints.

This research had the responsibility of creating tasks which could be assessed by up to 25,000 teachers in a valid and reliable manner. The subject's generic practical nature, coupled to its multi-disciplined structure made the task uniquely different from those in other subjects. Three types of assessment activities were produced:

- contextual practical tasks assessed by outcome;
- prescribed practical tasks differentiated by task; and
- tests.

The question was how well each achieved the requirement to differentiate pupil achievement in a fair yet consistent fashion. In the event, political intervention fuelled by teacher hostility was the key factor in determining the avenues of research pursued.

The first National Curriculum in Technology had five attainment targets, four of which related to design and technology and one to information technology. In National Curriculum jargon they were known as Te1 to 5 – Te1 to 4 were the attainment targets for design and technology, and Te5 information technology. All pilots and trials aimed to determine each pupil's level of achievement in each attainment target. For comparative purposes and to determine a subject score, attainment target scores were aggregated. Much debate and research was undertaken to determine the weighting given to the four attainment targets. However, final decisions about weighting matters were generally subjective and driven either by the politics of the subject or broader policy decisions.

Contextual practical tasks assessed by outcome

This style of task was used during the first two years of the research. The tasks were typified by a highly resourced activity based on a context. Each had similar resources for teachers and pupils which provided a standardizing framework. In particular, every pupil constructed their response around a set of identical labels which operationalized the assessment criteria in a practical pupil-oriented manner. The three tasks used in the pilot were the fourth version and these had gradually evolved over a 24-month period with input from a wide variety of sources (teachers, LEA advisers, academics and HMI). They represented a curriculum interpretation of the Technology Order of 1990, offering access to all pupils regardless of the resources and specialist facilities at their disposal.

Nearly 10,000 pupils took part in this trial and the mean level of attainment achieved was 3.2. As the first National Curriculum had ten levels of attainment, and level 3 was indicative of 8 and 9-year-olds, this was alarmingly low for pupils in Year 9. There were though, sound reasons for this mean performance level. This type of task required pupils to perceive a need or opportunity from one of three specified contexts; consequently, the range of activities undertaken was numerous. So did the context affect performance? Would it be fair in statutory assessment to have a range of contexts, or alternatively would it be unfair to only have one? If the mean profile components are considered, the performance on the three tasks varied from 2.95 to 3.26. The difference between the highest and the lowest is 0.31 of a level, approximately 10 per cent. There is no way of determining if this is an acceptable degree of variation and perhaps it is rather irrelevant. However, it was important that every pupil had the opportunity to achieve their best level of performance, regardless of the context. Correlation with teacher assessment is the best way to assess this aspect, however, teacher assessments were not wholly reliable, as they had been made only for research purposes, and were frequently based on how the pupil had performed in the assessment task, a somewhat tautologous situation.

Were the contexts fair in relation to gender? If the mean profile components are examined by gender it is clear that boys and girls performed better in different contexts. The original intentions envisaged a bank of tasks which could be used for statutory assessment purposes. If this had occurred, the evidence argued for the provision of more than one context, but perhaps, only if the pupil is allowed to choose. This approach would have raised serious management issues which teachers, during the infancy of the National Curriculum, did not manage to resolve. In addition, the effect of the management structure employed by a faculty or department on pupil performance was probably significant. With time the most efficient approach would have emerged and become models of good practice or means of achieving good end of Key Stage assessment performance.

What is remarkable is the similarity of performance in relation to the attainment targets, regardless of the task or of gender. This offers further support for the notion of a bank of tasks. Both boys and girls achieved the lowest levels for the task with the most demanding technical content. If choice were allowed, pupils and schools might opt for contexts which were technically less demanding. This could result in a bias away from these aspects of the programme of study. To avoid this, these results could be regarded as scores and performance means could then be standardized regardless of the task taken. For example, each task might have an associated difficulty factor or tariff. This procedure might be acceptable for comparing say, school performance, but would make nonsense of reporting an individual's performance. It would, however, allow a school the opportunity to select the task which fitted their programme rather than selecting the one which superficially seemed the easiest. This would also necessitate the disassociation of school accountability from pupil performance at the end of Key Stage 3.

Prescribed practical tasks differentiated by task

In the pilot the tasks were differentiated in relation to resource context, typically the material base (e.g. food) in which the pupil would tackle the task. Structured process diagrams at three bands of difficulty also provided pupils with different objectives. This model was further refined for the first statutory assessment. In each material the task was specified at four levels of complexity. In this model the behavioural criteria, the statements of attainment, were combined with outcome goals derived from the programme of study to produce assessment criteria based both on process and product. These tasks only sought to assess Te2 and Te3. This approach was not deemed fair by the nation's design and technology teachers as it was only offered in three materials: construction, control and food. This was a bureaucratic decision which, rather unfortunately, provided a focus for criticism and greatly affected teachers' attitudes to the whole process. It should not be seen as a commentary on the structure developed for this task. This model, with some modifications, was employed for the subequent tasks the following year. The introduction of two other materials, graphics media and textiles, overcame much criticism and the tasks were generally well received.

The initial provision of five tasks based on specialist facilities produced mean profile components which ranged from 4.1 (food and textiles) to 3.7 (construction and control). The aspects of the subject traditionally associated with girls produced the highest levels of attainment, and those associated with boys the lowest. The mean profile component for all pupils for all tasks was 3.92. The variation between highest and lowest is 0.4 of a level, approximately 10 per cent. This performance does clearly illustrate that girls outperformed boys; this occurred in all trials and pilots of practical tasks undertaken during the period of this research. This is confirmed by noting that of all pupils taking food and textiles, 65 per cent were girls, whilst of all those taking construction materials and control 58 per cent were boys. There was further evidence which identified a possible area of unfairness. Teachers reported that pupils required significantly more time to complete tasks in construction materials than in the other areas. This also affected control since it required pupils to use similar materials in making a solution. If tasks are set in relation to different materials then there is a sound case for establishing a different rubric for each task. There is also considerable data on the relative performance of the genders. From the evidence presented it would be sensible to conclude that girls outperform boys in all aspects of design and technology capability. However, it is possible that the emphasis placed on pupils to record their progress discriminates unfairly as it rewards those who are conscientious in this respect. There was substantial evidence that girls placed much greater value on this aspect of their work and were consequently rewarded.

The task-differentiated tests produced for use in the first statutory assessment were trialled, due to the need for confidentiality, in a limited way in the preceding year. The trial required teachers to enter pupils according to four different tiers and three different tasks. The mean level for the attainment targets being assessed was 3.7 for both Te2 and Te3. This was the first time that Te3 had not produced the highest performance figures, but it was the first time pupils had to undertake tasks which had to meet specified performance criteria. Performance varied between the tasks, more so than in previous trials. Teacher interpretations of the control task caused significant underachievement in this respect, whilst performance in the food task in respect of Te3 was far higher than in the other two tasks. Teachers did not relish entering pupils in particular tiers, they believed that their decision was placing a ceiling on each pupil's possible level of achievement. Whilst acknowledging that at the end of Key Stage 3 the levels of pupil performance could vary considerably, teachers did not wish to bear the responsibility of deciding which of the differentiated tasks would provide the appropriate challenge for each pupil.

Tests

Tests were introduced to assess attainment in relation to Te1 and Te4. The statements in these two attainment targets were not intended to form the basis of a test. Strategies had to be devised which would enable this to be achieved. These evolved from questions which required the assessor to judge whether a pupil's response satisfied a statement to questions in the pilot, to ones which were marked for the pre-statutory trial and the statutory assessment in the following year. In the first instance, various aggregation rules could be applied to decide, on the basis of the statements satisfied, what level had been achieved. In the second, the marks obtained at each level were totalled, and the highest level at which these equalled or surpassed a pre-established mastery level was the recorded level of achievement. In the pilot all pupils entered at the same tier took the same test, but in the statutory assessment pupils took tests which were linked to the practical task taken.

The shift from asking the examiner to make a single judgement in relation to a criterion to a marking system was evidence that criterion-referencing was not easily applied to the construction of traditional paper and pencil tests and the way in which they were marked. Even if questions could be set against the criterion, teachers did not feel a marking system which only allowed a question to be marked right or wrong was fair. Marking allowed some reward for answers which were not wholly accurate, for example, when the pupil had not fully evidenced the statement being assessed, but had partially met the criterion. Once the notion of marking and levels of mastery was introduced the system was also open to calibration. As Angoff (1974) noted quite correctly: 'if you scratch a criterion-referenced interpretation, you will very likely find a norm-referenced set of assumptions underneath' (p. 13). Simply by making comparisons to any criterion-referenced assessment, one is making a norm-referenced interpretation. For example, if it is expected that pupils should typically be achieving between level 5 and 6 by the end of Key Stage 3 and the tests had mastery levels, the level could easily be adjusted to ensure that nationally this norm was achieved.

Did the tests differentiate pupil achievement and, if so, was this achievement related to design and technology or was it dependent, for example, on skills relating to comprehension and expression? Possibly the best answer is found by examining the correct response rate to questions. Performance graphs showed clearly that response rate declined as questions became more difficult – 73 per cent successfully answered level 1 questions whilst only 26 per cent were successful at level 10. Surprisingly, the test scores increased pupils' performance by 0.42 of a level, even though these two attainment targets only accounted for 35 per cent of the weighted subject score. An analysis of performance by practical task taken also revealed that the test was fair regardless of the task taken.

The tests first trialled adopted a marking procedure with eight marks being available at each level. A key task in the trial was to determine at what level the mastery should be set for each attainment target. There was no reason why mastery levels should have been the same for both attainment targets, or even for the section related to each practical task. It would though have been exceptionally difficult to have convinced teachers that different levels were fair. The analysis of this trial showed that response rates to the questions differentiated achievement quite perceptibly. Is it possible to determine fairness when pupils were taking completely different tasks and tests? Was anyone in a position to decide if the assessment procedure relating to food was as difficult or easy as the construction or control material tasks? If fairness is equated with similar performance distribution possibly the only option is to calibrate, by adjusting the mastery levels following marking. But these levels had to be decided long in advance of even the tests being taken. Such an approach would also have resulted in a truly examination context for what had started out as classroom tasks. Deciding on a mastery level prior to the tests being taken illustrates the dilemmas this type of assessment posed. Compared to GCSE, which some claim is a criterion-referenced examination, where calibration and grade decisions are taken post testing and marking, the situation is very different. At GCSE grade boundaries are set at different points for different examinations depending on pupil performance.

Were the tests fair to pupils? Initially, for the first cohort, it is unlikely that they could have been. For many, the first test of this nature which they would have taken would have been the statutory test; any argument which claimed that inexperience created a fair context would be dismissing each pupil's right to demonstrate their best achievement. Once again, timescales proved to be the greatest obstacle to fairness. If pupils and teachers had been aware of the assessment process when they embarked on the Key Stage then tests of this nature would have had a greater degree of legitimacy. Each of these three assessment modes has the same objective: to produce a subject score. From a political perspective, all that was required was a number for each pupil which could be aggregated to produce a school, local education authority or national average. This performance score could then be monitored on an annual basis and improvement detected – comparative, norm-referenced judgements. What was required was a summative score, but many might mistakenly interpret the score in relation to the assessment criteria. Just because the initial assessments were criterion-referenced, it cannot be assumed that *post hoc* generalizations about the skills and knowledge mastered by a pupil achieving a certain level would be reliable. For example, does a pupil who has obtained a profile component of level 5 understand all aspects of the programme of study at that level, and has he or she achieved all the statements of attainment in each of the attainment targets up to this level? Such conclusions should be treated extremely cautiously, as the subject score is far removed from the assessment decision, especially if the criteria have been subsumed into a scheme for a test which has been marked.

Conclusion

The research demonstrated that each of these procedures does discriminate achievement. Whether these procedures were or would have become fair is more difficult to determine. If pupils had secure and reliable teacher assessments, performance correlations would have provided definitive conclusions. Where comparisons can be made, for example, mean aggregated performances are very similar, but analysis has not been undertaken at the pupil level. For pupils to demonstrate their best achievement the evidence indicates that there should be choice. This would need to be in relation to the context or the material base depending on the nature of the task.

Although hypothetical, because both the National Curriculum has been revised and design and technology is no longer subject to statutory assessment, which of these procedures might have provided a model for the future? Tasks initiated via a context were deemed to be the most appropriate way of assessing Te1 but since this imposed significant demands on management, it is unlikely that even with time and experience it would have been acceptable within a statutory regime. The style of task trialled does though provide a good model for teacher assessment. Level-differentiated practical tasks available in an appropriate range of materials do have the potential to assess Te2 and Te3 in a statutory framework. This style of task could also have included Te4, which would have provided a fairer and more relevant assessment of this attainment target. A short paper and pencil test of Te1 which was common to all pupils would have completed the testing process. With weighted attainment targets, 85 per cent of the assessment would come from the practical task and 15 per cent from the test. This would reflect accurately the very practical approach adopted by the majority of Key Stage 3 teachers to the teaching of the subject. Any increase of the weighting towards the test would distort the subject for pupils of this age.

Subsequent revisions, despite opposition, have maintained the criterion-referenced approach but with the emphasis moving from the attainment targets to the programme of study. In time, it is possible that teachers will appreciate and recognize the value of criterion-referencing. The setting of performance goals is of value to the teacher in motivating pupils and recognizing and rewarding achievement when it occurs. But there must also be recognition that this has implications for a formal assessment context in which reward is not always possible for partial achievement. Level-differentiated practical tasks would be the most appropriate means of assessing design and technology in a statutory way.

This chapter provides a detailed and informative record of the development of criterion-referenced assessment statutory assessments in design and technology at Key Stage 3 between 1989 and 1993. It established a range of strategies and approaches applicable to the assessment of design and technology regardless of the context; many have already been utilized in GCSE examinations. Until the past fifteen years the assessment of practical, process driven subjects, such as design and technology, has been largely neglected. The thesis from which this chapter has been drawn will add to the subject's expanding literature by bringing into the public domain research which might otherwise have been unavailable as a resource for future researchers.

References

Angoff, W.H. (1974) 'Criterion-referencing, norm-referencing and the SAT', *The College Board Review*, **92**, p. 12.

Gipps, C.V. (1994) *Beyond Testing – Towards a Theory of Educational Assessment*. London: Falmer.

Glaser, R. (1963) 'Instructional Technology and the Measurement of Learning Outcomes: Some Questions', *American Psychologist*, **18**, pp. 518–21.

Goldstein, H. (1994) 'Recontextualising Mental Measurement', in *Educational Measurement: Issues and Practice*, **13**(1), p. 42.

NCVQ (1991) *Guide to National Vocational Qualifications*. London: National Council for Vocational Qualifications.

Resnick, L.R. and Resnick, D.P. (1992) 'Assessing the Thinking Curriculum: New Tools for Educational Reform', in B.R. Gifford, and M.C. O'Connor (eds) *Changing Assessments: Alternative Views of Aptitude, Achievement and Instruction*. Amsterdam: Kluwer.

Chapter 9

Distinctive Skills and Implicit Practices

Richard Kimbell, John Saxton and Soo Miller

Introduction

This chapter is based on a three-year research project investigating 'Design Skills for Work' undertaken at Goldsmiths' College for the Design Council. It is focused on the radical changes taking place in the contemporary view of design and the training of designers; the distinctive (and transferable) skills that designers possess; and the pedagogic paradox that is currently devaluing design in higher education (HE).

Context

Design has never before held such an influential position within popular culture, and there have never before been so many students studying design on degree courses in higher education. Our research examines these courses – and the skills that are acquired by students on them – but before embarking on an account of the research, it is necessary to contextualize the issues we will raise by outlining the dramatic transformations that have overtaken both design and higher education in the last few years.

Design in transition

Design theory and its reflection in practice has changed as our society has moved from the industrial to the post-industrial and from the modern to the post-modern. Throughout the twentieth century, modernism in design has been associated with opportunist designers adopting highly rationalist views of their role in society. As Margolin (1989) argued, engineer-designers like Behrens and Buckminster Fuller, and design educators like Gropius in the Bauhaus and Maldonado in the Hochschule in Ulm:

> all believed that advances in science and technology were evidence of social progress and provided paradigms of design thinking. They thought that communication could be objective and that optimum solutions to design problems could be found . . . design, rationally conceived, could help to solve social problems and did not itself create such problems. And most assumed that goods should be mass produced by industry.
>
> (Margolin, 1989, p. 10)

This ethic of design created a non-contentious role for designers in society:

> Conventional designers can be considered timid, because they have accepted the role of auxiliaries to production. They remain intermediaries between consumers and producers, interpreters of specifications that have mainly been drawn up by other people . . . (whilst) philosophers and moralists have shown a concern for politics; very few have concerned themselves with design. In their minds designers are mere actualisers or draughtsmen giving material shape to ideas generated elsewhere.
>
> (Moles, 1989, p. 77)

The issue that has changed this rational, modernist view of design concerns the relationship between the designed object and people: in particular, the recognition that objects do not have fixed meanings that are the same for everyone, and that designing is better characterized as creating a dynamic relationship between the object and the user. The supposed universal values underpinning modernist design are replaced by individualized values.

Design 'training' in transition

Design training has moved progressively away from art schools and in Britain is now located principally in faculties or schools in the former polytechnics that now comprise the new universities. This realignment brings new pressures to bear on design training. Traditional art school practice valued individual talent, placing the fine art ethos at the centre of training for designers and crafts persons. The tradition remained as these studies moved into faculties of art and design within the new polytechnics and universities, and design teaching now finds itself in a new position in which long-held values and traditional practices are equally under threat.

Many would argue that the designer has for too long been taught in isolation, devoid of interaction with other disciplines and the potential of a broader university environment. The designer has not typically grown up alongside, rubbing shoulders with, the businessman, scientist or engineer. However, the location of design teaching within a broader university environment has slowly brought about the beginnings of change. Contact between disciplines has developed both informally and through the development of cross-discipline and modular courses, and the resiting and gradual reorganization of subject disciplines in the new universities. Modular programmes and networks are no longer focused exclusively on a single discipline but embrace the common processes of design thinking that are found across all design activity. Eighty per cent of institutions now offer modular design programmes (Temple and Morris, 1995) and as these programmes provide greater levels of flexibility, the question that is increasingly being asked is whether at undergraduate level students should continue exclusively to be trained as professional practitioners. Is (should) a design degree be a purely vocational experience?

Mass higher education and the growth in student numbers

Higher education has expanded enormously in recent years with now some 1.3 million full-time students. Resources have not followed the growth in numbers and traditional forms of teaching, particularly in workshop and studio-based subjects, are facing inevitable change. Designers have traditionally been taught through studio and workshop practice under the guidance of individual tutors (the atelier model); an expensive and labour-intensive form of teaching. In the best British tradition, many faculties of art and design have struggled on and papered over the cracks, but the drive towards mass higher education (with the dramatic increase in student numbers) has brought this method of working to virtual breaking point.

The pragmatic pressure for change exists at the same time as (and in parallel with) an increasing body of opinion arguing for a more liberal concept of design education: a concept of design for all; design as general education. State schools have, quite properly, aimed to teach the underlying processes of designing and have adopted a general, non-vocational approach to design teaching, looking at the broader issues of design activity, technology and the role of the consumer. This stands in stark contrast to practice in higher education which has been mainly concerned with vocational training rather than education, concentrating traditionally on the preparation of a single-subject, talented specialist who will find employment in a limited job market.

> The vast majority of students interviewed aspire to practise as designers in their chosen field, and that remains the rationale behind their choice of programme.
>
> (Temple and Morris, 1995, p. 51)

Moreover:

> Many educationalists consider that it is no longer valid or appropriate to train people specifically for one career function . . . an expectation that any one student will remain in the sector in which she or he trained is no longer accurate.
>
> (*op. cit.* p. 51)

The corollary to this is that the numbers of students graduating in narrowly conceived design programmes does not equate with the numbers of jobs available in that specialism. Whilst at one time art schools aimed to match student numbers with employment needs, this is no longer possible, and there is a *prima facie* case for design courses to place increased emphasis on the more broadly educational responsibilities of undergraduate study, and on developing the generic skills and flexibility needed in an ever-changing career.

Students can no longer afford to have fixed ideas about employment. What we are currently witnessing is the growth of the concept of the 'portfolio career', where jobs do not exist 'out there' in some monolithic design industry, but rather are more transitory and dependent upon the individual talents and aspirations of creative young people.

The response of design educators

The principal message from this analysis is that an exclusively vocational rationale for design in higher education is no longer tenable. What is required is the development of a genuine design discipline.

> We can imagine what a legal scholar might contribute to the profession of law ... (but) we still have little understanding of how a design scholar might be able to bring theory, criticism, or history to bear on issues central to the design professions, whether these issues relate to practice, education, or even public perception of design and designers.
>
> (Margolin, 1989, p. 4)

This issue lies at the heart of a research project commissioned by the Design Council in 1997 and conducted at Goldsmiths College, University of London. This project centred on design skills and their value in the workplace which, for the purposes of this project, was defined as embracing all paid employment and not just employment in the design industry. The central question was *What skills and qualities do design graduates possess that make them valuable to employers – any employers?*

The project raises many difficult issues, not least the conceptual problems of discussing 'transferable', 'generalizeable', 'core' or 'key' skills for employment. These matters were explored in *Design Skills for Work* (Kimbell *et al.*, 1998) and used as the starting point for an empirical study of practice in higher education design programmes. In association with the Design Council, we identified and approached a number of design courses in HE institutions across the UK (with a spread across graphics, product, engineering, interior, textiles, fashion, and design studies). In each case we interviewed the course tutor responsible for the *second* year of study – partly because the second year represents the most intensive and representative teaching year and also because it is the year immediately adjacent to student placements (where these applied). Three students from each programme were interviewed as a group (they were chosen by the tutor to best reflect the philosophy and practice of the programme). The aim was not to examine *all* practice but rather to explore the extent to which, and the ways in which, these courses recognized, valued and developed design skills so as to render them portable into diverse employment contexts. We are most grateful to these tutors and students who gave willingly of their precious time and talked frankly and with enthusiasm about their work.

The tutor interviews (approximately 90 minutes) concerned the distinctive 'identity' of the course, the characteristics and qualities developed by students during the course, the selection criteria for recruitment, the teaching pedagogy, the role of placements within the course, and the skills and attributes developed through design practice. The student group interviews (approximately one hour) focused on why they chose to study design at university, why they chose this particular course, the design skills and qualities they brought to the course, the skills and understanding they had developed on the course, and what they thought were the particular qualities they needed to get a job when they graduated. Supplementary documentation from the courses was used to contextualize the data from these interviews.

A conceptual framework for considering design skills

There is a paradox at the heart of this study, for whilst it may be true that design skills have a *general* usefulness, it is equally true that if they are acquired on design tasks then they are learned in highly *specific* contexts. Design is fundamentally concerned with the particular. Kimbell *et al.* (1998) argued for a framework elucidating design skills which are acquired and practised through highly particularized and contextualized tasks, but which, once learned, are transferable to other tasks and to domains outside of the world of design.

We identified some of the categories of designerly performance that we believe are of significance, and placed them on a spectrum that describes these skills as operating at the *strategic interface* between, on one hand, abstract higher-order intellectual intentions, and, on the other, particular, functional, prosaic skills that are used to express and make manifest these thoughts and intentions. This is illustrated in Figure 9.1.

Designers simultaneously inhabit all three sectors of this spectrum since they are simultaneously driven by motives and intentions that are operationalized through strategies and realized through skills. However, we concentrated on the middle-order operational strategies because, as we argue below, it seems to us that the uniqueness of design is best described here.

At the abstract end of the spectrum, *any discipline* can claim to develop the ability to be, for example, *evaluative*, but we have sought to

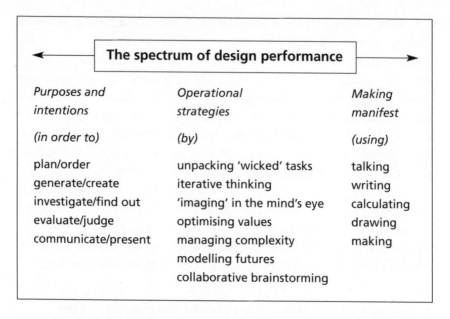

Figure 9.1 *The spectrum of design performance*

put flesh on these abstract capabilities by indicating the characteristic (and frequently unique) strategies that designers use to translate these intentions into outcomes. Equally, we do not believe that the functional skill domain best captures the essence of design because this domain essentially comprises the tools that give external form to our thoughts, and all disciplines use such modes of expression. We believe that the special qualities of design and hence the general value of design education exist in the central strategic group of the spectrum.

Our framework goes considerably further than more generalized frameworks for transferable skills for employment. Whilst The Secretary's Commission on Acquiring Necessary Skills (SCANS, US Department of Labor, 1991) talks about developing 'creative thinking' and 'problem-solving', and Allen (1993) talks of 'autonomous learning' and 'teamwork', our framework identifies some of the specific strategies that designers use to achieve such qualities.

In order to validate this claim, we examined the empirical data emerging from the design courses in our study. How do tutors teach design skills? To what extent do students see themselves developing a robust and transferable battery of strategies that are not only applicable in a design context, but equally in any other area of employment?

Distinctive skills

Both tutors and students provided powerful evidence about the development of designing strategies. Since there is not space to consider the whole spectrum in our framework, we highlight five of the central ones that proved to be intimately related – unpacking 'wicked' tasks, optimizing values, modelling futures, coping with risk, and managing complexity.

Unpacking 'wicked' tasks

In our draft report (Kimbell *et al.*, 1998) we discussed the 'wicked' nature of design tasks. They are wicked in the sense that, typically, they are

- individual (each is unique);
- have no definite formation;
- have no stopping rules (i.e. development can just go on and on);
- cannot be true or false;
- have no complete list of operations;
- are capable of multiple solutions; and
- have no definitive 'truth' test.

It is a very real challenge therefore simply to get to grips with such a task. What is it? What are its components? How might it be approached? Unpacking the task not only reveals the complexity but also enables the student to identify and focus on the central issues and other concerns that need to be addressed:

> How you unpack a task, how you take it apart, is done in lots of different ways. There is a focus on students' understanding, stripping it right down to the bare essentials and then putting it back together with something that wasn't there, so they get a better understanding of it.
>
> (student and tutor interviews)

This capability is complemented by the designers' ability to keep the task at the forefront of their thinking and continually revisit it, refining and redefining their understanding of it, and consequently their design proposals to meet it. Unpacking tasks is an active ongoing capability:

We keep going back to things when we are designing: we always revisit. We keep going back to the brief.

(student and tutor interviews)

Optimizing values

Design is not just about change, it is about *improvement*, and the concept of improvement is essentially value-laden. Good design practice therefore seeks to identify the stakeholders in any task and make their values explicit from the outset. Any designed object is the manifestation of a set of values, and making this relationship explicit is the first step towards optimizing a design solution. The outcome of design activity must not offend the values of those who commission it or those who are perceived as being the purchasers of it, and arguably, the closer the designer can fit the outcome to the value positions of the principal stakeholders, the more successful it will be judged. The problem for the designer is that there will seldom be unanimity in this regard, and that is where the optimizing skills of the designer come to the fore:

> They learn that design is not an egocentric activity – it is doing it for others, understanding needs, ethical and moral.

> It's absolutely about other people and not about themselves. We encourage positioning . . . for people that don't necessarily look at the world from their point of view.

(student and tutor interviews)

Modelling futures

Part of the problem of dealing with 'the new' or with 'improving' the present is the fact that it is very difficult to make the necessary judgments if we cannot first create a realistic simulation of effects and impact (what it is like and how well it will work). Even if we have clarified and prioritized the values that will apply in making judgments about a developing product, it is impossible properly to evaluate it unless we can examine it as a 'virtual' reality through modelling.

As designers, we continually model our concept of a potential future state to enable us to experience it vicariously and thereby make informed judgments about it. The closer this vicarious experience can simulate the ultimate reality, the better we will be able to judge its impact in the new reality when it is realized:

> they are testing the future.

> you've got to be able to model . . . to give you an insight into whether its going to work or not.

> if you have a mock-up you can turn it around and put a hole in here or there or whatever . . . to see how it works.

> Ultimately they would develop them into prototypes but en route, there are a series of staging posts when we would like them to model their concepts . . . the concepts could be in any form or medium to communicate the idea.

> It's very, very important . . . you can simulate complex situations.

> It is very much about modelling the future, and about restructuring.

> (student and tutor interviews)

Coping with risk

Design is all about the future. It is about creating objects and states that do not yet exist and that are therefore, to some degree, uncertain and unknowable. This uncertainty creates risk. The capability to simulate, and hence evaluate the consequences of a design – by modelling – allows the designer not just to be innovative but also to be able to manage the risk that is always inherent in the new and the innovative. Modelling is therefore not only a powerful tool for designers, it is an invaluable tool for any decision-maker. It underlines the imperative of determining the effects and consequence of ideas *before* commitment. Innovation and risk go hand in hand, but the designer learns to manage and control the risk through modelling:

> We deliberately reward risk – what we are really rewarding is creativity, which is risk.

> You have got to have failure – because if you don't fail you will never transcend.

> If you are going to reward risk then you've got to reward failure as well.

We are saying – I'm better a glorious failure than a boring success.

We want them to challenge what's going on and take it further . . . we allow them to take risk, we allow them to experiment. I think it helps them to confront failure.

(student and tutor interviews)

Managing complexity

This issue again goes back to points raised earlier concerning the 'wickedness' of design tasks. Such tasks are typically multi-dimensional, messy and value-laden, and designers have to optimize solutions bearing in mind competing priorities. They have to take a project from inception to completion, often over an extended period of time. They have to manage their resources, and the appropriate supply of materials and equipment, in ways that enable them to complete their task. At the end they typically have to bring together all the strands of thought and development into a single holistic solution. They need to be holistic integrative thinkers whilst managing the messy and often contradictory strands of thought within a project:

I think time management is a big thing . . . some manage time by the skin of their teeth, others are more methodical. They manage six different tasks in one semester. They start at the same time and the deadlines are the same for all of them. Time management, project management, when to do research, etc. are all important.

Management is one of the most important things. Working to a deadline is important, no matter how well organized you'll get to the deadline and think 'if only I had a bit more time', so you have to organize your time because if you don't your design is going to get worse and worse.

Rather than going down the pub and drowning your sorrows, I suppose subconsciously you can step away from a problem and put all your concentration into something else, then you can come back to it fresh having taken your mind off it but still being productive.

(student and tutor interviews)

One of the inevitable ingredients of a design task is uncertainty, and this too needs to be managed. Students learn to manage themselves through projects, often starting with constrained and limited tasks and gradually working towards larger and more imprecise tasks. Much of the learning centres on the management of the activity, developing a plan and a schedule, checking and amending it at regular intervals, trying to iron out factors over which one has less control and maximizing those over which one has more control. Managing uncertainty is a critical design skill:

> From setting a design task to presenting it is all about handling uncertainty.
>
> (student and tutor interviews)

The solution to any design problem may not involve conceptually difficult material, but it is very likely to involve highly complex and interrelated levels of planning and decision-making. In short, designers learn to handle complexity and uncertainty.

Summarizing the skills

We have an enormous quantity of evidence that underpins the position we outlined earlier, that the distinctive features of a design training and the capabilities that students acquire are best described in this central category that we have termed 'operational strategies'. They are neither high-level abstract ideas, nor are they purely functional skills. Rather, they operate between the two as strategic and operational. Specifically, this research suggests that at the heart of design capability lies a set of strategic skills that our students acquire through design experiences:

- the ability to unpack and get to grips with highly complex tasks;
- the ability to recognize and optimize value positions;
- the ability to model alternative futures;
- the ability to cope with risk;
- the ability to manage complexity.

These are exactly the skills that SCANS (US Department of Labor, 1991) and Allen (1993) describe as being central to employment in the modern world. Not just *design* employment, but *all* employment. Our analysis of the interviews we have conducted with students and tutors on a wide range of design courses persuades us that these students are well equipped to demonstrate exactly the skills that employers need. They have been learned through very specific design contexts, but they are nonetheless highly relevant and transferable into any employment context.

Talking with tutors and students to tease out this distinctiveness, we became ever more conscious of the paradox to which we referred earlier. These distinctive strategies are immensely empowering and highly portable to many contexts, tasks and circumstances. But we became increasingly aware of the fact that the design students themselves did not see them in that way, and the consequences of this are serious, as we outline below.

The vocational tunnel

There is absolutely no doubt that *all* of the design programmes within our sample were conceived as serving vocational purposes. The tutors see themselves as training their students to be designers in various disciplines and fields, and the students are quite clear that they are training to be either specialist or generalist designers, working somewhere in the design industry. They do not see themselves pursuing a higher education degree in the classical sense; rather they are training for a specific profession and in the main they have an occupational route planned:

> For me it doesn't have to be product design. I wouldn't mind seeing how interiors worked and maybe even furniture.

> What I would ultimately like to do is work with a number of employers like a freelance consultant.

> We all plan to go into design.

> (student and tutor interviews)

However there is a harsh reality that begins to dawn on the students as they work their way through the course – there are not jobs for everyone. The design industry is simply not big enough to absorb them all, even within a widely cast net of the creative industries. One recent estimate puts the figure as low as 2 per cent gaining direct design-related employment, but MORI (1998) estimates the value to be closer to 20 per cent:

> Our findings show that students are optimistic about obtaining a career in design, but not realistic . . . 78 per cent of students who

want to work in a design-related career say that it is likely that they
will do so after completing their education.

(MORI, 1998, p. 12)

By the end of their course, many of these students are becoming
somewhat more realistic as the reality of their career opportunities
becomes more apparent to them:

> There is a notable variation in views on employment opportunities
> in design by year of study. Final-year students are more realistic;
> approaching half agree that there are few design-related jobs,
> compared to a third of the first year students.

(MORI, 1998, p. 13)

As graduates from other disciplines, so many design graduates will seek
employment in occupations not related to their specific studies – in
finance, insurance, retail, manufacture, service and community work. In
fact the chances are that more of them will become these things than
will become designers.

Perhaps this is not so bad, however, for our evidence suggests that
design graduates have developed an awesome variety of skills that they
can deploy in pursuit of whatever employment is available. But herein
lies the rub. For it seems that students in the main are astonishingly
unaware of the range and scope of the skills they possess.

Design – an all-embracing label

Many of the qualities that tutors require of students, and which we have
seen demonstrated in their work and through our interactions with them,
are embedded in this entity called 'the design process'. A whole panoply
of skills is subsumed within, and seen as implicitly part of the process
of designing. The skills are not articulated as identifiably discrete elements
of capability. Accordingly, to take just one example from our discussions
with students, despite the fact that 'research' is a skill at which they are
very accomplished (since all projects involve lots of it), they do not see
themselves as appropriately qualified to apply for a research post (for
example, on a newspaper or at the BBC).

The issue repeatedly encountered during fieldwork concerns the
prevailing pedagogy on undergraduate design programmes; a pedagogy
that has the design process at its core. There are two versions. On one

hand, in the traditional *atelier* model, the process in the main is *not* articulated; rather, its organic 'messiness' is founded on talent and absorbed through contact with a practising designer to be fostered in the greenhouse studio environment. On the other hand, in more contemporary design programmes, the complex thinking processes of designing *are* articulated, but they remain located in a highly focused design context. Both approaches, however, fall short of delivering an education that has employment currency comparable with other undergraduate programmes because, ultimately, the students on these programmes are blissfully unaware of the important skills and qualities that they possess.

The pedagogy problem

Our discussions with students revealed that whole catalogues of skills are seen merely as integral parts of the process of designing. When asked to say what qualities and skills they thought they might be able to offer to an employer outside the design industry, they talked only about personal qualities (e.g. determination) and interpersonal skills (e.g. teamworking). For a significant number of the students interviewed, the realization that they held other generic, transferable, and highly marketable skills only began to dawn on them as we talked. This is an important issue and it brings us back to the key role of the tutor and to the pedagogy underpinning the course.

On some programmes the whole experience of the course is shrouded in mystery. Tutors launch interesting and challenging projects without making clear to students what they are learning, or why they need to learn it. It is seen as a composite, organic experience. There is almost a level of deliberate obfuscation on the part of tutors:

I don't think we ever articulate that . . . it just happens . . . sometimes it dawns.

They don't ask for anything; they take things on trust.

I don't think they are aware of that (tutors' pedagogic planning). It just happens . . . I think the whole thing should be a sort of game . . . if you actually told them this is what happens I don't think they would learn it in quite the same way . . . because by learning it . . . they are discovering it for themselves. I don't think they realise half.

I've never actually articulated that to myself, but I guess that's what we are doing.

(student and tutor interviews)

This is the truth of it. Students fail to realize how skilled they are, or that their often outstanding designing ability can actually be marketed as a glittering array of talent and expertise that has applicability well beyond the world of design.

On programmes that do articulate thinking processes there is a clearer understanding of the designing process, but it is still seen as a complex, multifaceted whole in which many of the contributing skills and capabilities are not recognized as discrete qualities.

Conclusion – the metacognitive imperative

It is one of life's ironies, that those who have developed capability are not necessarily conscious of the skills they are using. They may have become embedded in their practice and, in terms of the designer's priorities, may become almost entirely subsumed into a concern for the production of successful outcomes. The issue we are concerned with therefore is to do with 'making explicit'. Design degrees have developed on the whole under the auspices of the art school tradition with a teaching methodology that, in the main, is not articulated. Many of the students we interviewed had an impressive range and variety of skills that have general use in many areas of human endeavour. However, the students were not consciously aware of building these skills for themselves and consequently they were able to do little more than describe them as integral parts of the process of designing.

Part of the problem with this lack of explicitness is not just the lack of awareness in the student; it also relates to other people's (employers') perception and understanding of the skills and capabilities of design graduates. It is more than just about the student's own perceptions of these qualities; it is equally about public awareness.

The evidence of our study is that the multitudinous skills of the designer are used tacitly, which is of little benefit to students who need to be far more aware of the new skills they are developing. They need to consciously stop and think about what they are doing and how they are doing it in order to develop an understanding of the power of the skill and the ways in which they personally can operate it successfully.

All this speaks to the need for students to become aware of the skills and qualities they hold.

Student design portfolios might be seen purely as product development tools, helping students to externalize their ideas in order to communicate and discuss them with others. Ideas, reasoning and decisions are not kept internal in the mind, but rather are externalized as language, images, models and objects, and this explicitness is central to the value of the design experience. However, to be valuable as a learning experience, the strategies being used need additionally to be liberated from the immediacy of the design task, allowing students to reflect on them as part of a metacognitive framework of capabilities.

Effective learning requires awareness of one's own processes – not just being able to do it, but being self-aware as one is doing it. This metacognitive imperative sits at the heart of any effective pedagogy, since all learning requires that students are aware of what they are learning. This is why Schön (1983) talks of the 'reflective practitioner'. If we seek to develop expertise in others, it is no good simply being good ourselves. We need to understand *why* we are good in order that we can introduce these features to others. All too frequently the students we interviewed tended to see the skills and qualities we have outlined in this report as part of an overall design capability. They could not articulate them as individual skills or qualities.

This is not to suggest that the prevailing pedagogies of these programmes need to change radically, since tutors are successfully developing in students a wide range of skills. But at least in one regard these courses do need to change. Design tutors need to make explicit through their planning and their pedagogy the skills and qualities they are seeking to develop. By articulating them, they will become part of the day-to-day discourse and will progressively empower the students. The strategies identified in our framework need to be *explicitly* identified and *explicitly* practised so that they become part of the metacognitive armoury of an effective designer. If they are not made explicit, if they remain as tacit practices embedded in thoughtless routines, then there is no reason to believe that the skills will become embedded as robust and transferable.

There is no reason to believe that students will (of their own accord) make the jump from working on *particularized* design tasks to the formation of a robust conceptual framework of *generalized* design strategies. Whether they do or not is not to do with design. It is to do with the ways in which design is taught. The key pedagogic factor is the explicitness with which these skills are debated and developed.

Design is in a transition from being seen merely as the intermediary between producers and consumers to becoming a principal contributor to the definition of our culture. Design education is in a parallel transition from being merely a vocational training programme for industry to being a powerful learning medium that enables students to develop the strategic, innovative, intellectual, personal and interpersonal skills that are increasingly sought in so many areas of employment. The best measure of the success of a design degree should not be how many students gain employment as a designer, but what diversity of employment opportunities are opened up for that majority of design graduates who will not be designers.

References

Allen, M.G. (1993) *Improving the Personal Skills of Graduates – A Conceptual Model of Transferable Personal Skills*. Sheffield: Sheffield Employment Department.

Kimbell, R., Saxton, J., Miller, S., Green, P., Liddament, T. and Stables, K. (1998) *Design Skills for Work: An Exploration of Transferability*. London: Design Council.

Margolin, V. (ed.) (1989) *Design Discourse*. Chicago: University of Chicago Press.

Moles, A. (1989) 'The Comprehensive Guarantee: A New Consumer Value', in V. Margolin (ed.), *Design Discourse*. Chicago: University of Chicago Press.

MORI (1998) *Survey of Design Undergraduates*. London: Design Council.

Schon, D.A. (1983) *The Reflective Practitioner: How Professionals Think in Action*. London: Temple Smith.

Temple, S. and Morris, L. (1995) *Design Degrees. An Investigation into the Teaching and Learning of the Design Process in Higher Education*. London: Design Council.

US Department of Labor (1991) *What Work Requires of Schools – A SCANS Report for America 2000*. Washington DC: US Government Printing Office.

Chapter 10

Learning Through Making: the Crafts Council Research

*John Eggleston**

Making a product, usually three-dimensional, is at the heart of design and technology – it is the creative experience resulting in a tangible object which makes the subject different from others for the student. For the teacher the added dimension is the enhanced learning experience that making delivers.

These features, though widely recognized by teachers in many countries, have seldom been demonstrated by research. The Crafts Council, as part of its concern with making, decided to address this elusive area and invited three British universities to research it. This chapter reports the genesis of the project, the results of the three research teams, the overall conclusions and the ensuing recommendations for teachers, teacher trainers and examination and curriculum bodies.

Introduction

The Learning Through Making project began as an act of faith by the Crafts Council. It believed that intelligent and insightful three-dimensional making is one of the most dominant human activities in Britain today, and one that is integral to our national priorities for the future of the economy, employment, education and cultural wellbeing. Yet it is best known only at the margins. At one end of the spectrum are

* John Eggleston was rapporter and editor of the final research report from which this chapter is drawn. The permission of the Crafts Council to use the material is gratefully acknowledged.

about 25,000 highly talented artist craftspeople and designer-makers whose work often graces exhibitions, galleries and collections. At the other are the legions of 'do-it-yourself' enthusiasts and hobbyists. But in between is a vast range of 'makers'. Some use material to model vehicle prototypes, create television and film sets, or to build equipment and maintain our life support systems from houses and hospitals to food production. Others use practical intelligence to visualize, design and administer the industrial systems on which our society depends.

Why this research?

The Crafts Council was well aware of the vast constituency of makers which it serves and represents. But, in addition, it saw an urgent need to examine the central learning role played by making – not only in learning the skills to overcome the well-documented famine of competent makers, but also in learning life skills – in schools, higher education and through adult life. It realized that the contribution was only incompletely recognized, and its potential even more rarely appreciated.

The Council recognizes the value of craft activity for learning by direct experience at all levels of education. Making is a creative process that develops skills and competence by engaging with ideas and materials. Knowledge and understanding acquired through 'learning by doing' allows young people to enjoy a sense of achievement which will sustain a lifelong interest in the made world.

Creative and practical skills developed in education can provide valuable experiences which will support the national economy and improve the quality of everyday life.

Launching the project

In the light of these arguments a major research initiative on learning through making was established. It defined making as 'a creative process that develops practical, conceptual and visual skills through personal engagement with tools and materials in response to human needs' (Crafts Council, 1998, p. 3). Specifically, the Council wished to provide authoritative evidence to explain the benefits of learning through making at national and local level throughout life in the home, workplace, community and environment; and for careers of all kinds where practical action is required.

The Council also sought to discover if access to practical experience in formal education was valued by students, employers and society. Key questions included: *Has the school curriculum supported or hindered the development of creative practical skills and the understanding of the made world? How do art, craft and design graduates contribute to the economy in a post-industrial age? What are the implications for future policy-making in creative and cultural education and working life?*

In drawing up these questions the Council was able to use the findings of a national survey of making in art and design and technology courses in secondary schools undertaken for it at Roehampton Institute. The juxtaposition it found between the evidence of high student potential and problematic course delivery caused widespread concern.

The Council was able to finance three teams of researchers from Loughborough, Middlesex and Sheffield Hallam Universities. This chapter summarizes the main outcomes achieved by the research teams that examined different aspects of the programme.

The outcomes

Middlesex University

The team from Middlesex looked specifically at the results of learning through making and the ways in which human competence and capability may be enhanced by the experience. The researchers also attempted to measure and evaluate the experience. They looked at the context of education from ages 5 to 16 in each of the four Key Stages of schooling. They then examined how employers, many of them international, viewed these competences and capabilities. Finally they sought to explore how the general public regarded them. Research techniques included observation, interviews and questionnaire data analysed using the Statistical Package for Social Science (SPSS).

An important outcome was evidence of the closeness of the relationship between the making skills children were able to acquire in school and the practical competences desired by the children themselves and by employers. There was also useful evidence of enhanced all-round learning that came with the experience of making.

It was apparent that the full range of competences and capabilities arises quite 'naturally' even though they are rarely the focus of teaching and learning objectives. Teachers do not have to invent appropriate tasks or situations; capability in a practical making environment automatically demands them.

Teachers involved with younger pupils more consciously used making as a central strategy in a programme of work because it enabled them to stress the development of personal qualities, attitudes and cognitive abilities. At secondary level making was implicit in almost all subjects. Although teachers' first concerns were subject competence, almost all consciously used making to help in the development of psycho-motor coordination and physical organizational skills.

The competences which comprised both the employers' and teachers' 'wish list' could be summed up simply as practical common sense and productive capability. They included:

- ability to cooperate;
- ability to communicate when doing things;
- conscientiousness, honesty, reliability;
- initiative, energy, persistence and self-discipline in tasks;
- acceptance of responsibility;
- ability to comprehend through listening, reading and doing;
- job-specific skills;
- problem solving;
- adaptability in changing circumstances;
- application of knowledge in the solution of practical problems;
- ability to handle factual information;
- the capacity to view problems from different angles and perspectives;
- motivation in the accomplishment of tasks;
- ability to organize things and people;
- ability to think logically.

The report confirms and lends authority to the convergence of the 'cultural understandings' of educators, employers and the general public, and emphasizes the distortions caused by the persistent academic dominance of education from nursery through to university – a dominance which leaves making and learning through making under-valued and under-used. Most of the practical capabilities and competences that many of the adult respondents most valued and enjoyed had to be learned after their formal education at work and during leisure time. Whilst they appreciated the limited opportunities for making that schooling had given many of them, what they keenly regretted was their brevity and low status. They perceived the current National Curriculum as exacerbating rather than alleviating this situation.

A further important finding of the Middlesex team was to emphasize the three-dimensional aspect of learning through making. The team found little evidence of the same beneficial consequences in computer-assisted design and manufacturing. Whilst they emphasized the importance of Computer Assisted Design (CAD) and Computer Assisted Manufacture (CAM) as crucial components of modern making, they saw the key benefit of learning through making as springing from the actual use of materials to generate a product.

Loughborough University

The Loughborough University team explored in detail the experience of making in education, and in particular the development of understanding of how materials, technologies, processes and wealth generation occur in human affairs.

The report found abundant evidence of the enhanced understanding associated with making but, like the Middlesex team, reported that very much of the learning occurred in adult working life and leisure time, and that the opportunities for developing such an enhanced understanding in schools were, at best, only incompletely realized. They reported that:

> A huge range of skilful craft-based areas of activity is pursued by adults. Many of these, even if not well recognized 'officially', support considerable specialist communities and have their dedicated journals and associations. On this view, craft knowledge, craft-based activity and craftsmanship are alive and well. The future is, however, less promising: they are now less well supported in the schools' curriculum.

Making (or intelligent making) is not sufficiently well expressed in the National Curriculum Key Stage 1 and 2 documents to represent its educational significance; nor is it expressed in a way that is entirely appropriate to Key Stage 1 and 2 education. Key Stages 3 and 4, biased towards industrial production, also insufficiently engage pupils in meaningful making.

Secondary school pupils enjoy 'practical making' provided it engages realistically with their motivation and aspirations. They do not appreciate what they see as 'irrelevant theory' and 'paperwork', regarding neither as being necessary in the 'practical learning' of 'practical subjects'.

The language in which programmes of study are couched pays scant attention to the educative developmental functions of making, and little or no attention to the educative potential of craft knowledge, the crafts, craft-based activity, and the development of aesthetic qualities and sensibilities.

The team also found that intelligent making is fundamental to human development in all its aspects – it is a practical and a necessary mode of knowing and understanding. Craft-based activity provides exemplary opportunities for intelligent making.

Craft-based activity provides satisfying career opportunities, contributes significantly towards the leisure and tourism sectors of the economy, and provides considerable satisfaction via engagement in specific craft-based activities and in DIY.

Sheffield Hallam University

The Sheffield Hallam team focused on the employability of craft education graduates, the national and international demand for them, and their capabilities and developing roles as employees and employers. The team surveyed graduates and staff from six craft-based courses at higher education institutions ranging from jewellery and metalwork at Dundee to fashion and textiles at Brighton.

Like the Middlesex and Loughborough teams, the Sheffield Hallam team found evidence of the widespread enhancement of learning through making activities. Predictably, however, in higher education this was recognized and developed in the craft courses but only occasionally related to the non-craft courses, even though some obvious relevances could have existed, notably between craft and business studies placement.

The diverse destinations of craft graduates were dramatically illustrated in a diagram reproduced here as Figure 10.1.

The team reported that:

- their review of literature from a wide range of disciplines
  suggests that craft education could impart new styles of thinking,
  acting, flexibility and problem solving. These may be more

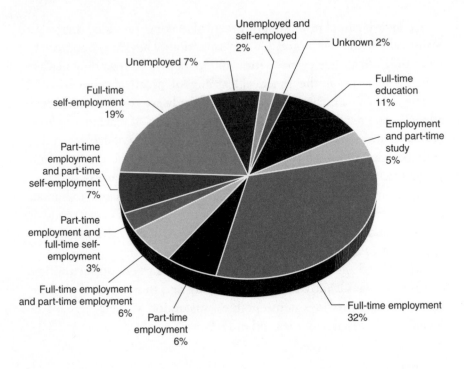

Figure 10.1 *Destinations of craft graduates*

appropriate than traditional learning systems in meeting the needs of a changing culture, including those of management and the professions;

- their survey of the employment patterns of craft graduates broadly supports this view. The idea that craft education leads to high unemployment, or that the only tenable 'proper' jobs are in art and design teaching, are both clearly refuted. So too is the out-of-date paradigm of the craft practitioner as 'the lone potter';

- of those who are employed or self-employed, 75 per cent work in art and design-related fields. There is also significant employment in management professions and a clear trend for craft graduates to be employed in management some years after graduation;

- art and design-related self-employment is a significant recent destination undertaken by 20 per cent of respondents. A diverse range of creative making and design activities is in evidence, including work for the film industry, other performance arts and the retail sector;

- half of all respondents are engaged in multi-track careers. Multi-tracking self-employment with paid employment, two or more part-time paid jobs, and two or more forms of creative practice are all in evidence. Those most likely to be multi-tracking are people in full-time paid employment who supplement their employment and lifestyle with some part-time self-employment activity;
- the project-based approach to learning in craft, involving the management of time and multi-tasking, appears to equip people with the confidence and skills to develop multi-track 'portfolio' working. With over half of all respondents working in this way, craft graduates are perhaps at the forefront of developments in the restructuring of work and leisure.

The findings of the Sheffield Hallam, team, like those of the other teams, closely relate to those of an independent report on graduate employment by Heskith (1998). This confirms that the skills most highly valued by employers include self-reliance, teamworking, communication, problem solving and the ability to learn quickly and individually – all characteristics demonstrably delivered by graduates in the Sheffield Hallam survey. However, Heskith makes other points corroborated by the Hallam study; that the employers with the lowest skills requirements are also least satisfied with the skill levels of new graduate recruits, and that 'employers may not be optimizing their use of graduate skills within their companies' (pp. 62–3).

Findings

Drawn together, the findings of the three projects give rise to the conclusions discussed here.

Learning to make and learning through making are seen as key components of contemporary education by employers, the general public, educators and students themselves. They are regarded not just as desirable parts of lifelong learning, but as necessary for the individual, occupational, social and family life of the community. Words such as observation, perseverance, accuracy, achievement and satisfaction were frequently used to describe the experience and the achievements that learning through making was able to offer. The researchers thus reiterate the findings of

Dearing (1993) and almost every major public report in the past two decades.

Employers across the board value general practical competence and welcome evidence of this in both individual selection and career progression. This is quite apart from a desire in many industries for specific training and practice competence which has a direct relevance for the work in hand. It is rather a more general appreciation of adaptability, but being able to see assignments through, having three-dimensional conceptualization, and many other more general professional skills.

There is a close relationship between making ability and employment. Qualified students (especially graduates) were very successful in obtaining work in craft-related industries, starting up businesses, and succeeding in the management and administration of a diverse range of new and established enterprises. This occurred even though the employment of some craft and design graduates initially appeared modest or unsuccessful. As in many creative industries, notably music, the gap between accreditation and successful employment was variable, but this in no way diminished the ultimate achievement of most of the craft and design graduates surveyed.

Members of the general public value their making experience at school highly, frequently citing it as the trigger for engaging in practical hobbies such as DIY and community projects with voluntary organizations. They also believed that being able to think in three dimensions helped them as consumers, home-makers, garden-planners and in many other aspects of their working life and leisure.

Creative practical learning can offer a major contribution to the widespread desire to make education at all levels relevant to everyday life. In real terms, this includes school links with community projects and work experience, industrial placements and 'live projects' in higher education, core components in GNVQ activities and links between art, craft and design courses and business and marketing.

Making activities can enhance teachers' enabling roles, particularly with pupils who need special support and assistance. In the close personal relationships that making activities promote, teachers are able to give more personalized, guided and visible opportunities to enable students to assess their own progress. Moreover, teachers were unanimous that making a model, working on a three-dimensional project, or creating a mechanical device almost always enhanced learning of scientific and mathematical concepts in particular.

Educators, whether directly engaged in teaching and making activities or not, showed high regard for learning through making, but commonly regretted that its recognition had a low priority in Britain. They saw an urgent need to enhance the status of learning through making, both through changes in the National Curriculum and the examination and accreditation system, and subsequently in the admissions procedures adopted by most universities.

Craft activity is poorly supported in the school curriculum. Intelligent making is seldom explicit at Key Stages 1 and 2 and there are limited opportunities for 'live' projects and aesthetic development at secondary level (Key Stages 3 and 4). There was a tendency in many schools to see learning through making as largely the responsibility of the Design and Technology and Art departments, but the evidence suggests that this responsibility can and should be located across the curriculum.

In some schools, making was seen as being delivered through information and communication technology. Although ICT is now an essential part of learning to make, it is only one component of making. Without the experience of materials and actual production it is insufficient and inadequate.

Drawing attention to the difference between computer skills and practical skills, Suzi Leather, a member of the RSA Focus on Food Campaign, commented that while 85 per cent of primary school children can now use a keyboard, only half that number can chop carrots or peel potatoes.

National Curriculum changes have reduced the number and type of school-leaving examinations which make a true assessment of making capability.

Finally, in many schools a 'making gap' occurs after age 16 or even at 14 where art and design, and design and technology is wholly or partly discontinued after Key Stage 3. This means that many skills are often not developed or maintained before entry to employment. This is particularly worrying as this is the time when young people develop physical control and coordination.

Recommendations

The findings gave rise to a long list of recommendations to schools and teachers, teacher trainers, and curriculum and examining bodies. These include:

To schools and teachers

1. That intelligent making activities should be enhanced and made regularly available to all pupils across the curriculum, at least until the end of full-time schooling so that they may develop practical skills and imagination.

2. That whilst making activity should include a full understanding of ICT, it should be recognized that ICT alone is not a substitute for the whole experience of making.

3. Concentration on literacy and numeracy should not detract from a balanced, integrated and reinforcing scheme of making activities which not only develops ideas, spatial perception and dexterity, but also problem-solving and related analytical, language and numeracy skills.

4. All schools should ensure that they maintain an adequate and appropriate resource base for a wide and appropriate range of realistic making activities.

5. That schools make every opportunity, including the use of training days, to increase the practical making competence of their teachers.

6. That schools make arrangements to have makers in residence in similar ways to the writer and artist in residence schemes that currently exist in many schools.

7. That schools should ensure close links between design and technology and art and craft departments.

8. That school-leaving examinations should be carefully chosen to ensure full recognition of making capability.

To teacher trainers

1. That personal making skills in initial teacher training be emphasized more strongly for all entrants to teaching, as a national curriculum for teacher training is developed. Teachers should be able to identify opportunities for making, deliver them and evaluate the outcomes.

2. That skilled making in a range of materials and design contexts should be an important part of in-service training provision for primary and secondary teachers.

3. That a system of awards for distinguished teachers be adopted,

with capability in learning through making being one category
of such awards.
4. That urgent measures be adopted to resolve the serious
shortage of new design and technology entrants to teacher
training.

To curriculum and examining bodies

1. That the making component in the National Curriculum be
emphasized more strongly both in art and design and in design
and technology, as well as in a full range of other subjects
where three-dimensional understanding is likely to be
beneficial such as history, geography and science.
2. That National Curriculum revision takes this need into urgent
consideration.
3. That the practical making component of GNVQ and NVQ
programmes, especially in manufacturing, art and design, be
reappraised and extended.
4. That care be taken to recognize making capability in
appropriate school-leaving examinations.
5. That the 'skills gap' in the post-16 school curriculum be closed
as part of a broader post-16 curriculum. This is particularly
important to ensure a well-prepared and qualified flow of
entrants to further and higher education art, craft, design and
technology programmes.

Epilogue

This chapter has presented research in yet another different way. It is
targeted not at researchers or teachers but at those who make decisions
about the subject – governments, ministries, official agencies, and those
who determine the curriculum, teaching, assessment and examination
of the subject. The findings of the three projects commissioned by the
Crafts Council are presented clearly and directly, targeted to officials
and administrators who are not required to study the research or to
pursue the references although they are available if required.

This form of research presentation is now strongly advocated by the
British Educational Research Association which has long been frustrated
by the lack of attention given by policy-makers to conventional research

reports. The issue is fully discussed in BERA's journal *Research Intelligence* of March 2000 where Bassey (2000) distinguishes between academic and various user reviews of research.

However, this chapter makes a fitting finale to this book because, with only minor adjustments, many of the recommendations could derive from any of the researches reported. Design and technology education needs research urgently but it also needs consequential policies and delivery. Research must take an active role in the development of our subject.

References

Bassey, M. (2000) 'Review of Education Research', *Research Intelligence*, **71**, 22–29.
Crafts Council (1998) *Learning Through Making: A National Enquiry into the Value of Creative Practical Education in Britain*. London: Crafts Council.
Heskith, A. (1998) *Graduate Employment and Training towards the Millennium*. Cambridge: Hobson.
Leather, S. (1997) *Chairperson's Introduction*, Focus on Food Conference, Royal Society of Arts, Halifax: Design Dimension.
Loughborough, Middlesex and Sheffield Hallam Universities (1998) *Destinations of Craft Graduates*, presented in an unpublished research report to the Crafts Council. Incorporated into Crafts Council (1998).
SCAA (1993) *The National Curriculum and its Assessment (The Dearing Report)* London: School Curriculum and Assessment Authority.

Index